UNAPOLOGETIC GOSPEL

AND

UNAPOLOGETIC KINGDOM LIFESTYLE!

DR. MELVIN C. RHINES SR.

DR. ANDREA P. RHINES

Scripture quotations taken from the Holy Bible, King James Version, New Kings James Version, New International Version, Amplified, Amplified Classic Version and The Message Bible. Copyright © by International Bible Society. All rights reserved.

Published by Andrea Pamela Rhines Publishing

© Copyright 2020 by Dr. Melvin C. Rhines Sr. and Dr. Andrea P. Rhines

ISBN: 978-0-578-71014-3

Table of Contents

Acknowledgements:

We give all glory to YAHUAH, YAHUSHA AND OUR HELPER, THE RUACH HA'QODESH! We thank all of the people for their contributions and prayers that helped us in our process in the writing of this book!

However, as it is written:
"What no eye has seen,
what no ear has heard,
and what no human mind has conceived"—
the things YAHUAH has prepared for those who love him—
1 Corinthians 2:9 NIV

Introduction

Our Heavenly Father YAHUAH inspired us to write this
book, "UNAPOLOGETIC GOSPEL AND
UNAPOLOGETIC KINGDOM LIFESTYLE." He said,
"Tell them about my goodness." For we are YAHUAH's
[own] handiwork (His workmanship), recreated in
YAHUSHA HA'MASHIACH, [born anew] that we may
do those good works which YAHUAH predestined
(planned beforehand) for us [taking paths which He
prepared ahead of time], that we should walk in them
[living the good life which He prearranged and made ready
for us to live]. (Ephesians 2:10 Amplified Classic)

When we obey our Heavenly Father YAHUAH, it gives us
a life of abundance and overflow of all good things.
YAHUAH gave us His principles, laws and wisdom in His
written Word to live a victorious, overcoming, and
triumphant life.

The results of following YAHUAH's Word and The
RUACH HA'QODESH's inspired direction will lead you
to a life that YAHUAH has for your purpose and destiny.
We settled in our hearts to follow YAHUAH's plan for our
lives, not our own plans and ideas. He promised to meet

every need, and He did in abundance full of love, joy, peace and prosperity. "Now to Him Who, by (in consequence of) the [action of His] power that is at work within us, is able to [carry out His purpose and] do superabundantly, far over and above all that we [dare] ask or think [infinitely beyond our highest prayers, desires, thoughts, hopes, or dreams]. (Ephesians 3:20 Amplified Classic)

You are about to embark on a journey with us that will increase your faith in YAHUAH's ability. You will discover the favor of YAHUAH as never before, and you will become more deeply and intimately acquainted with your Heavenly Father so that you will be able to receive YAHUAH's best for your life and ministry. You will be inspired to give YAHUAH total control of your destiny.

Our suggestion to you is to read the Cepher Bible.

Chapter One

~ ~ ~ ~ ~ ~ ~ ~ ~

Discovering YAHUAH's Plan

One day, as I was laying on the couch, I kept asking YAHUAH, "What is my purpose on this earth? What do you want me to do?"

Then I heard a small voice in my ruach say, "Television!" It seemed strange, but I knew it was our Heavenly Father YAHUAH answering me.

At the time, I had a business called Andrea's Creative Concepts. I developed self-esteem and diversity workshops for companies. I had started the business, of course, to generate income, but I also wanted to be on the same schedule as my children. This time period was truly happy for our family. I had met all my business goals. My husband, Melvin, had a strong career and he was accomplishing his goals. Our two sons were healthy and happy. Our marriage was strong, we liked the area where we lived, and we went to a place of worship we loved. We had serving YAH like I had always wanted. Life was indeed wonderful.

Occasionally I would look at myself in the mirror and wonder, "Why would YAHUAH want me to do television? Why me? Surely there are other people more qualified than I am to do television." I would just look at myself and say, "Well, He must see something I do not see."

Three years went by. Our third son was born. We were so happy. Melvin had always wanted more children. Now we were graced with another boy for "our team," as people had begun to say. However, we needed more living space, so we talked about what we wanted in a house. We prayed and started looking for our new home, and YAHUAH answered our prayer with exactly what we wanted!

We moved into a five-bedroom house with a fireplace, central air, a two-car garage, an office, two bathrooms, a deck, a family room, and an eat-in kitchen. All this came with no down payment, no closing cost and affordable monthly payments. Our Heavenly Father YAHUAH is such a good ELOHYIM!

I began to feel a tremendous tug to start working on the television show YAHUAH had told me about. I started talking with people in the television business. Until then, I hadn't felt YAHUAH leading to move ahead. But now the tug wouldn't let me work on my workshops without thinking about the television show.

I told Melvin I didn't know what was wrong with me, but I couldn't continue my workshops without working on the television show. Our Heavenly Father YAHUAH kept prompting me to begin. Melvin knew I was uncomfortable with the whole idea, but he was supportive and gave me the go-ahead to follow my heart. I started going to workshops about television and other areas of the media. I read magazines and books on the media. I also talked to people in the media business.

I told some of my friends I wanted to do television. They also were supportive and told me I would be good at television. My friends said I was warm with people and knew how to make everyone feel comfortable.

The more I shared what our Heavenly Father YAHUAH had told me, the more confident I became. The clear vision of my television show started to manifest. I started to get a good feel for the show and what I wanted it to be like, a talk show about the positive things in the community. It would also have a diverse appeal. With so many misconceptions about different cultures, our Heavenly Father YAHUAH wanted me to show people what I was accomplishing in my workshops. People are very visual. My show would tap into that quality by letting people see and experience others in a fun and good way. I knew our Heavenly Father YAHUAH wanted me to continue the reconciliation I was achieving in my workshops. This would be reconciliation on the air.

I knew I needed to write down on paper what I wanted to do. As I talked to different people, someone told me about a lady who loved to write and would do a good job of stating in print what I wanted for the show. I told that lady what I wanted, and she put exactly what I wanted in print. This allowed me to share my idea with others.

The idea was to have a television talk show with people about positive things going on in the complete community, all social and ethnic backgrounds, and I would host the show.

We would have segments with teens, cooking, fashion and adults with positive solutions to things going on in the complete community. The more I talked about the show the more people would tell me whom I needed to talk to for production ideas.

That was when I met a man who knew a lot about the television business. Talk about being led! YAHUAH was certainly putting me in the paths of the people I needed for the show. I could not believe what was happening. I thought, so this is what people are talking about when they say, "YAHUAH led me." YAHUAH is so awesome.

I knew I wasn't doing any of it. I had no idea what I was doing, I just obeyed YAHUAH! I just started talking and asking questions. The next thing I knew, the man was saying, "Let's do a television show!"

We started interviewing people, not for television but to practice and see what we really wanted. I went many places and talked to many people. I went to meetings in the community to share the idea with other people, and incredible things started to happen. I suddenly knew that I was to slow down and get the business side of things done. I told Melvin we needed a business plan, and two or three days later he came home with a friend who not only helped us develop our business plan, but also set up our corporation for our production company.

Melvin had not seen this friend for years, and they just happened to run into each other at the post office. Melvin simply told his friend what we were doing, and his friend had the information we needed. We know our Heavenly Father YAHUAH led Melvin to go to the post office at that particular time. I say that because we started to notice how things started to happen for us. Life hadn't been like this before we started doing the television show! We were on the right path. To research the industry, a friend of mine helped me watch all of the television talk shows. Then we decided what the show would and would not have.

I met a businessman at a network meeting. He asked to see our business plan and when he saw it, he was so impressed that he gave us an office space downtown! It was the biggest office in his unit, a complete office! We had to furnish only a few accessories. We had a fax machine, telephone, copy machine, conference room, receptionist, and help from people in the other offices. We even had our own computer. Now, you know YAHUAH led us to this man. On the path YAHUAH has for us, there is all the provision we need!

We started to meet with other people to talk about the show and how we would do different segments.

This was all possible because we now had a conference room to meet in. Of course, we started to meet more and more people who knew how to produce a television show, and people who could help with other areas. YAHUAH just kept on showing up with someone we needed in every area. One person would tell us about another. The next thing we knew, we had a team of experts on media.

I would just look at everyone and I knew then how big our Heavenly Father YAHUAH is and how little I am. The meaning of "We serve a big and mighty ELOHIYM" came alive in me.

Our Heavenly Father YAHUAH was leading me in the path He had directed for me. My husband started to tell me how much faith I had in YAHUAH. I said, "I don't know how much of this is faith. I just know YAHUAH wanted me to do this, so I am doing it, but He is the one doing the work! I am just following Him." I only knew that YAHUAH was putting a lot of people in my path, and it was such an awesome thing.

After all, faith is trusting YAHUAH's direction. So, Melvin was right, as I came to realize. Because people thought I was personable, the name 'Person to Person with Andrea Rhines" was chosen.

One day I was in our place of worship and suddenly started to cry. But I didn't understand why. A powerful feeling was coming over me. I was starting to comprehend that this television show idea I had from YAHUAH was a calling on my life. I didn't say anything to anyone at the time about what I was feeling, but I knew it was a calling. I don't know how I knew; I just did.

After having all of these feelings, my show became a vision and a labor of love. It was no longer just a good idea from YAHUAH. Somehow, I just trusted YAHUAH. I don't know how I just trusted YAHUAH, but I did. My husband said I had a special faith, but I didn't think so.

My husband didn't understand how I could simply know YAHUAH wanted me to do something and then just do it. I told myself, "Well, He is YAHUAH. If He doesn't know what is best, who does?" YAHUAH had answered prayer for me many times, so I figured I could do what He wanted me to do. It only seemed natural to me.

Meanwhile, our producer explained to me the concept of getting sponsors for the show. Sponsorship is standard practice in the television industry. It is giving people credit for what they do for you. In short, sponsors give you something in return for advertising, or television exposure of their products and services. The offers to sponsor our show was tremendous! People sponsored our trademark, our business cards, our stationary, folders, my entire wardrobe, makeup, and our furniture for the set. You name it, we got it. Our Heavenly Father YAHUAH is a very good ELOHYIM!

Call to Me, and I will answer you, and show you great and mighty things, which you do not know.
Jeremiah 33:3 NKJV

I met the designer of the television show in a specialty store. She was a clothing designer who shared time working in the store with several other designers. As I walked through the mall, the design in the store caught my eye, so I decided to stop in.

I introduced myself and explained that I was doing a local talk show and I needed a wardrobe for the show. She told me she would like to sponsor our show by providing her designs, and she would ask some of the other designers whether they were interested as well.

She called me back and said she and several other designers would be happy to provide my wardrobe for the show. She also helped with every area of our set design.

During the whole time, YAHUAH continually surrounded and blessed me with such wonderful people. Words are not adequate to express my gratitude to our Heavenly Father YAHUAH. It was also at this time that many unusual things started to happen to me. I would go to a specialty store and see something I liked, and the store owner would just give it to me.

Now I was starting to understand how YAHUAH gives you favor with people. This favor would happen a lot. For example, my designer would make something for her store and could not sell it. That particular piece of clothing would happen to be a piece I liked, so she would say, "This must be for you." He is a great and wonderful ELOHYIM I serve. I say this not because of all of the things He gave me. I say it because of who He is and how He is so faithful to provide for me.

For you, O YAHUAH will bless the righteous;
With favor You will surround him as with a shield.
Psalm 5:12 NKJV

During this time, some people told us we would not be able to get a show like this on the air. They said, "There are so many talk shows on the air already."

But we knew there was no talk show like this one. YAHUAH had already shown me how much He could do, and no one could talk me out of this now! They would have to talk with our Heavenly Father YAHUAH about it, because I was not listening. I decided I was going to keep doing what I was doing until YAHUAH told me to stop.

I was still doing my workshops, so I told our Heavenly Father YAHUAH I needed some help with my children. Melvin was in the military at the time, and he was out of town several times a month. I said, "YAHUAH, you have to get me some help or I can't do this anymore." Our Heavenly Father YAHUAH directed me to talk with my husband, and Melvin suggested putting an ad in the assembly bulletin for a nanny. Well, our Heavenly Father YAHAUAH did it again. Within a few days a woman answered our ad and again, she was exactly what we had requested. We had been very specific in our request. Melvin hadn't thought anyone would actually answer the ad. He had just gone along with the plan to look good in my eyes. But YAHUAH proved to be different. Our Heavenly Father YAHUAH was becoming more real to Melvin as well. YAHUAH gave me a live-in nanny who loved our Heavenly Father YAHUAH and my children. We shared the cooking, cleaning and the care of the children.

She was such a great help to Melvin and me. YAHUAH is a very good ELOHYIM indeed. He knows what we need and how to get it to us.

One day Melvin came home from work to a house full of people I had invited over. All the people present were helping with the show in some way. Melvin came into the house and could not believe what our Heavenly Father had done. It became very real to him then. He was both amazed and shocked. After that, Melvin decided we would put some of our own money toward the show. He wanted to do it because I had worked so diligently on the show. He knew it had to be YAHUAH working, because he knew I didn't know anything about television. I had a feeling that this was not just a call on my life, but a call on Melvin's life as well.

Many months went by, and I found out I was pregnant with our fourth son.

I thought not only was I producing and hosting a television show, but I also seemed to be producing sons. The comments kept coming now. Everyone thought we must be trying for a basketball team. But I assured them that was not my goal! I had so much energy during my pregnancy. Everyone talked about getting tired, but I seemed to have more endurance than everybody else. When they would be settling down, I would be gaining momentum. That was when I discovered how the anointing of YAHUAH's presence energizes you when you follow His plan.

One day I was coming home from the office and I heard in my ruach the name of the book. I went into the house, sat down on the chair and asked Melvin to give me a pencil and paper.

Then I started to write several pages of this book, talking about divine inspiration. All of this inspiration was flowing like a river! Melvin just stood there, looking at me as if to say, "What is she doing now?" After the flow of information stopped, I told Melvin, the title of the book. It is about how we started the television show.

I said, "YAHUAH, where do you get all of these ideas? Don't you know I have four boys, a husband, and I am doing this television show? And now you want me to write a book?" I thought, "Is He trying to kill me?" (I knew our Heavenly Father YAHUAH was not trying to "kill me." I used that phrase in the past when I felt overwhelmed, but no longer use it.)

Now, this may sound like the craziest thing you have ever heard. Here I was, telling Him how many children I had and what He had me doing, as if He didn't already know! What I couldn't understand is why He had chosen me to do all these things. But when I searched my heart, I knew one of the reasons was that I would do whatever He told me to do, even if I didn't understand. This is called a yielded heart, and I was totally yielded. If YAHUAH told me to do something, I would do it.

I didn't write anymore for a while, but now and then I would write a little more and a little more. I let a friend of mine read it and she liked it, so I kept writing whenever I was inspired.

I was such a happy little pregnant person. And I just loved what our Heavenly Father YAHUAH was doing with the show.

I was learning a great deal, and during my prayer time, wisdom kept coming from YAHUAH, showing me how to get things done. I loved being with our Heavenly Father YAHUAH! I would go for walks and talk with YAHUAH about why He had selected me. I would take time to sit in His presence. I would get such peace and a ruach of calm that would help my day along. If things started to get tense,

I would leave for a while, go on a walk with YAHUAH, and listen to His constant assurance to move forward. I would keep checking to make sure YAHUAH was still with me, that I had not left Him behind. I have always had a very ambitious attitude and have always liked the idea of being an entrepreneur, so I would check periodically to make sure it was our Heavenly Father YAHUAH leading, and not just me moving ahead without Him.

My friend and I continued to talk with people about sponsorship, and we continued to meet with all the people YAHUAH had allowed to cross our path. We would call our producer whenever we needed him to give us advice or attend a meeting with us.

During this time, a lot of people promised a lot of things. This was also when we started to understand that people didn't always do what they said they would do. We started to experience conflict and confusion. People started to say things like, "That is not what I meant, you misunderstood what I said." Then those people would not do what we thought they had promised to do. This dilemma caused delays, it seemed, and Melvin and I believed it made us look like we didn't tell people we worked with the truth. However, what we thought were delays were not delays after all. YAHUAH's timing is not our timing. Our Heavenly Father YAHUAH faithfully helped us through it all. That was when I learned that even though our Heavenly Father YAHUAH tells you to do something, you may still have complications.

We found a place to produce a promotional tape for the show so people could actually view pieces of the show and understand our vision.

When we started to show the tape, people would make such comments as, "This is so refreshing. What a positive outlook you have. You give people hope again." These comments came from people who had seen only what we had done for a few shows."

We found people who helped us prevail, and we continued on. But I noticed things were not as easy as they had been. There was a resistance now in different places that had not been there before. But we kept seeking YAHUAH and praying, and we continued with our plans to produce the show. Then we found a place to air the show.

After the show was produced, I started to hear more and more about the devil. I already understood about conflict and obstacles because I owned my own business.

People would say to me, "You have become a threat to him. He has taken notice of you." And this caused me to say, "Well, where have I been all this time?"

My husband and I started to read about warfare. We gathered all the information we could on faith in YAHUAH and the call on your life because people were starting to do things we did not understand. We knew that what we were experiencing was greater than minor obstacles and conflict.

We started to pray and read the Bible together more. We attended a Bible study, and we also held a Bible study in our home. We were accustomed to praying, but now we were studying the Word more and getting to know YAHUAH more. Melvin was in the military, so this looked a little like battle to him. However, our Heavenly Father YAHUAH kept us encouraged and moving forward with the plan He had placed in our hearts.

We started talking more about the station we wanted to air the show, when we wanted to air it, and what we wanted to accomplish with it. We made telephone calls to several stations and we found one station we wanted to pursue, so we made an appointment and took the tape to that station.

The lady at the television station liked our show and politely told us she would call us by the end of the week. However, she had called me by the time I walked in the door from our meeting with her. She wanted our show! We were so happy because she told us we could have the exact prime time slot we wanted. We were so excited because all of our hard work had paid off, and our Heavenly Father YAHUAH was so faithful to us during that time. He sent us to people to encourage us and to help with financing at the time others couldn't come through. It was YAHUAH who helped us to continue in that which He wanted us to do! What a trust I had in our Heavenly Father YAHUAH now, but not because of anything I had done. My trust came from our Heavenly Father YAHUAH showing me He is trustworthy.

You might wonder why I didn't tell you every detail of the trials we went through. One of the reasons is that our Heavenly Father YAHUAH told me to tell you about His goodness. He said to me, "Tell them about my goodness," and I am following through with what YAHUAH instructed me to do with this book. However, I don't want you to think we didn't go through trying times. We did! But our Heavenly Father YAHUAH always saw us through. Even when it wasn't easy for us, He made a way! We do not always know what is going on when YAHUAH gives us instruction to do something. However, if we stop and pray, He will give us direction!

Now we were ready to start production, and we decided we wanted a different set of furniture for our shows. I also asked our Heavenly Father YAHUAH where I could find some furniture. Then I got on the freeway, and I simply knew in my heart the direction I should go. I ended up at the place that had the furniture we needed. I had never met the manager of the store before that day. I just introduced myself to him and gave him one of our information packs, and he said, "Take whatever you want."

So, my friends and I went back to the store together to pick out our furniture. Again, it was the favor of our Heavenly Father YAHUAH. Where He sends, He provides. The manager told me he would deliver the furniture and accessories by Thursday, and this was Tuesday.

We also needed some trees for the set, so I went down the street to an accessory store and I showed them our promotional tape. They said we could have whatever we wanted but they didn't have a delivery truck, so I went back to the furniture store and asked them if they would also pick up and deliver our trees. They said yes! Now, how many companies would deliver someone else's merchandise? Not many!

It gets better. By the time I walked in the door at home, the owner of the production company was calling me to tell me the furniture was being delivered. I said, "They just told me they would deliver on Thursday." The production company owner responded, "well, it is here today." As we continued to talk, I found out that he had asked our Heavenly Father YAHUAH, whether he should produce our show there again. I think he got his answer. The delivered furniture had come as confirmation to the production company that they should produce the show.

During that time, we produced three shows. The owner of the production company told me our Heavenly Father YAHUAH performed many miracles while we were in production. Previously, the production company could not get certain accounts. However, during the production they received accounts that had not been available to them before. Our Heavenly Father YAHUAH again was putting His stamp of approval on the production.

Our designer did a fabulous job on the set and helped with so much encouragement. My friends and all of the talented production crew were wonderful. The production was very professional. I could not have asked for a better team of people, and my husband could not have been a bigger fan of mine.

I was in awe of YAHUAH and the working of His hand in our production. When issues arose, YAHUAH always provided a way of escape. One of the main challenges was the electricity. It went out for hours one time, but YAHUAH had given us the best electrical person on earth. We had our power restored better than ever. YAHUAH was always in control. We produced three shows that aired on a network during prime time.

Our Heavenly Father YAHUAH gets all of the glory for all of this. Without the hand of our Heavenly Father YAHUAH, we would have been totally stressed out and would have called the whole thing off.

We are so thankful to YAHUAH for his faithfulness. I think that during all of this, the hardest thing was trying to know whether we should stop or keep going. There was so much confirmation, yet that was also just as much conflict. I thought, "Is it YAHUAH's timing, or what?" I had always heard that if it is YAHUAH working, it will happen, so I thought everything should go smoothly. But that, I discovered, is not necessarily the way it is.

My brethren, count it all joy when you fall into various trials, knowing that the testing of your faith produces patience.
James 1:2,3 NKJV

This scripture seemed to have escaped my memory at the time because I kept thinking, "Is this YAHUAH's timing? Am I missing YAHUAH? What is going on here?" You see, I had heard so many different things that I couldn't figure out what was going on at first, or filter through the many voices. But YAHUAH brought me to the Word to confirm what was going on.

People were telling me, "Just because the door was opened doesn't mean it was YAHUAH." I was told to be careful. More things were said to me than I can even remember to tell you, so I simply said, "YAHUAH, you started this.

If you do not want it to happen, just tell me so." I figured if He started this, He certainly could stop it. I remembered something someone had said, "If you do not understand what YAHUAH is doing, trust His heart." I really felt the heart of YAHUAH in this situation. I certainly saw His hand in it, and that is why I continued on and finished what He told me to do. Our Heavenly Father YAHUAH is a good ELOHYIM.

The time for me to have my fourth son was approaching. It was time for me to get my house ready for the baby and to prepare myself for four children, so I took time off from everything and prepared for the arrival of my little bundle.

I started to spend a lot of time with our Heavenly Father YAHUAH and allow Him to heal me of some things that happened to me during the production of the television show. Do you know negative things try to hang on to you? I had to let go of some negative things that had been done to me. I had to make sure I took care of all the negative things that had happened with other people. I made some phone calls and apologized to people about the things that hadn't gone the way I thought they should have. I wanted to make sure they knew I cared about how everything had been handled.

Most people were very receptive, while others I wasn't quite sure about. But I wanted to make the effort, do my part, and let them know I cared about what they experienced.

A few days later, I went into labor and our fourth son, was born. We were so happy with him. Our family was now complete. My husband had two children before we were married, twins, a girl and a boy. YAHUAH knew I had wanted twins and Melvin had always wanted six children. We thanked our Heavenly Father YAHUAH for all of our children!

Our life was rich and rewarding, and I was very content just being a mommy and a wife. I would look around me and be amazed at what YAHUAH had given me. Our Heavenly Father YAHUAH will guide you through any situation you might have. Nothing is too hard for YAHUAH to get you through! He might not get you through as quickly as you would like but He will always bring you through.

I wanted to get to know the Father YAHUAH, YAHUSHA and The RUACH HA'QODESH better. I also wanted to do more for our Heavenly Father YAHUAH. I have always liked to read, so I read as many books as I could get my hands on about faith, prayer, and the Bible.

Melvin and I had more time together now, and we both had a desire to deepen our relationship with our Heavenly

Father YAHUAH. We had experienced so much of His goodness.

We visited a different place of worship during their camp meeting. They had preaching by ministers visiting from out of town. We had an awesome time. At the end of the camp meeting, something happened to me. I told Melvin, "I do not know if I can ever go back to our old assembly again." We visited the new place of worship, and we both had the same experience. We knew our Heavenly Father YAHUAH wanted us to move on to this new assembly.

We went back to our old place of worship several times to make sure this was YAHUAH. This need to change assemblies was unexpected because we had not been thinking about changing. We had not had a bad experience with our place of worship. We were content, loved our place of worship and what we were learning, and we loved our pastors. Melvin spoke with our pastor and he told us we were to go. He released us to move on to this new assembly.

Our old assembly had given us a good foundation for our marriage and our family. Our Heavenly Father YAHUAH wanted us to move on now for what He had waiting for us at this new assembly. YAHUAH does know what we need.

We were now rooted and grounded in our Heavenly Father
YAHUAH. We knew we wanted to live for Him always,
and that He had our best interest at heart. What a good and
gracious ELOHIYM we have!

We had a wonderful Bible study group at our old place of
worship, and we loved the group of people our Heavenly
Father YAHUAH had given us. We wanted to continue to
have a Bible study.

We had training, so we knew how to start a Bible study.
We just didn't know if our Heavenly Father YAHAUAH
wanted us to do this ourselves. He had prepared us for this
time by providing us the training. We had thought we were
being prepared to lead a Bible study at our old place of
worship, but we realized now that we were actually being
prepared to start a neighborhood Bible study. Our
Heavenly Father YAHUAH always prepared us ahead of
time, we just didn't know it. So, we started a Bible study in
our neighborhood.

We took turns meeting at each other's house, and our
Heavenly Father YAHUAH truly blessed our time together.
During this time our Heavenly Father YAHUAH continued
to increase our knowledge of Him and also helped us
understand why He had moved us to another place of

worship. He simply had things He wanted us to learn. He taught us that we are one body in MASHIACH.

It really helped us to be at the new assembly at this time. We had served in the ministry at the old assembly, and now at the new assembly we had to rest. The leadership told us to not do anything for six months. Just wait and see where our Heavenly Father YAHUAH would have you serve, they said. And this is just what we did; it was exactly what we needed with the new baby. We now had a little time to just be with our Heavenly Father YAHUAH. What a wonderful time we were having in our Heavenly Father YAHUAH. We were learning so much about destiny, purpose, and how our Heavenly Father YAHUAH will lead you into your destiny. We had felt that we were on the road to our destiny before going to this place of worship, but now we really knew we were on the road to our destiny.

YAHUAH had predestined us to be in this assembly at this time. We could really relate our situation to what our Heavenly Father YAHUAH had us doing.

We were so excited about our Heavenly Father YAHUAH and how He directed our steps to this assembly. We knew we were where our Heavenly Father YAHUAH wanted us to be. After our first six months, we knew we should be greeters at our place of worship, so that is where we served in ministry.

I began to feel like working again, so I started talking to people about workshops. Again, I thought more about the television show and what our Heavenly Father YAHUAH wanted us to do.

I prayed and asked our Heavenly Father YAHUAH about the workshops. I knew then that our Heavenly Father YAHUAH was not leading me to do workshops at this time. But we needed money, and I knew that our Heavenly Father YAHUAH knew we needed money. We were trying to understand what was going on, so we just continued to pray. We did not want to be out of the will of our Heavenly Father YAHUAH. But we also had bills to pay, and my income had always been there to help pay those bills. It was at this time that different things started to happen with Melvin's job.

Chapter Two

~~~~~~~~~~

Melvin's Journey

I started to see this call on our lives. I had thought of the
television show as a project YAHUAH had given my wife
instead of a call on our lives. However, so many things
started to happen that I had to look at it differently. My
wife always knew I would eventually have to come along.

I had been in the Air Force Reserves as an active duty
recruiter for the past ten years, and I was very comfortable
in my career. I had a steady, decent paycheck with good
rank. I was successful. I had received many awards and I
had good people to work with, which was a blessing from
YAHUAH. It had been rumored for several years that our
headquarters would be moving seasoned recruiters to hard-
to-recruit locations in other cities. The rumors got louder
and louder until it became a reality for me. During this
time, I had been praying to YAHUAH to not let this
happen, but I received orders to move. It came down to,
"You take this assignment, resign, or retire." My wife told
me she could not move because of the television show. She

left my decision in my hands. I had to listen to our Heavenly Father YAHUAH and decide what to do.

So I was trying to decide what to do. I thought about retraining for a new career field, but that would also require me to move, so I started to seek our Heavenly Father YAHUAH more than ever. I tried to ask my wife what to do, but she would not tell me anything.

She said I had to make my decision with YAHUAH's guidance. This was between our Heavenly Father YAHUAH and me; she was going to stay out of it. She knew I was the head of this family and this had to be YAHUAH working, not Andrea, and not me. My wife had talked with me previously about the business part of the production company for the television show. She said someone would have to make the decisions about the finances and if I didn't do it, someone else would have to because she could not handle everything. I didn't like the idea of some other person handling the finances, and she knew that.

During this time of seeking YAHUAH, the thought came to me, "Would it profit me more to follow my career desire or to follow the path our Heavenly Father YAHUAH had placed before me?" I talked with my pastor and he told me what he thought. I continued to pray and seek YAHUAH.

As I prayed, I began to know I was not to move to another state, so I retired from the Air Forces Reserves and found a position with the Army Reserves in our city. I could recruit and still keep the same rank. This was very exciting to me. I could have both! I could help with the television program and keep my rank and my good paycheck. I started the process of getting the position. They told me it was as good as mine, and I was happy. However, at the end of the process, they told me the position had been filled. How could this be? I was qualified, I had passed my test, and it was as good as done. What was going on? I couldn't figure it out.

I had to have a job, and I knew my wife was not supposed to do her workshop any longer because our Heavenly Father was leading her in the direction of the television show.

My wife had a feeling that I was not supposed to have a job in the military anymore, but she would not tell me that because she wanted to be sure it was YAHUAH working. She had a feeling that we were going to work together at this stage in our lives.

After that, I tried to get job after job, but the doors kept closing. My neighbor even told me I could have a job with him, but by the time I got to the interview, he told me the position had been filled. A friend of mine with whom I had worked previously hired me to do some work for him, which I did as long as he let me.

We were very confused at this time because I knew I needed a job. We went to talk with our pastor again. He listened, and then told us he believed we should follow the road of the television show. We found ourselves in the Bible all the time, trying to get answers and to make sure that what we were doing was scripturally right. We felt as though we were in school.

I continued to work for my friend. My wife and I would pray, take care of the kids, read our devotions, and pray again. Because of my career in the military and my travel, we hadn't spent a great amount of time together, and we now started to realize how much we had been away from each other. We had not realized how much we hadn't seen each other until I was home and no longer traveling.

I used to have an office in another state, so I would be gone for a week once a month. In between those trips, I would go out of town, and of course when I was in town, I was at the office all day.

My wife was used to not having my help. Now it was not easy for me to be around, trying to tell her what to do. I thought I was helping her, but she thought I was in the way. our Heavenly Father YAHUAH was working on our relationship and teaching us to work together. We didn't even realize we hadn't had much time together. I had trusted my wife to handle things at home because she had always done a good job of taking care of the kids, our home and me.

Now our Heavenly Father YAHUAH wanted us to grow up in Him and renew our minds to the way He wanted us to be. YAHUAH wanted us to become the new creatures the Bible talks about. He let us know our lives were going in a different direction. At this time, we started going to meetings to talk with people about sponsorship for the television show. We knew this was the road we were to take, and our pastor confirmed this decision. These sponsorships were vital in order to pay for the television show and to support our family.

Meanwhile, there was a pastor who lived down the street from us, who told me about an organization called Promise

Keepers. I told him I would like to volunteer, and he told me he would give my name to the person responsible for getting the volunteers. I was called to attend a meeting, and at that meeting I was selected to be an escort for the speakers. We had several meetings. I met men who loved our Heavenly Father YAHUAH, and that was so great for me. I enjoyed being with my wife, but it was also nice to talk with "the guys." The Promise Keepers meeting was awesome. Just being in a place with thousands of men who loved YAHUAH was remarkable, and I couldn't wait to do more for our Heavenly Father YAHUAH.

I had always dreamed of going to Africa. During a meeting about the television show, I saw African statues and pictures in a businessman's office. I asked him about them. He told me he had been to Africa and asked whether I had gone there. I told him it had always been my dream to go. He then asked me what was keeping me from going. I said, "My wife and finances." Well, my wife was with me at the meeting, and she said she would not care if I went. Remember, she was not used to my being with her as much as I was at this time, and I think she was ready for me to go somewhere.

Then the miraculous happened. The businessman said, "Your dream has come true. Your finances will be taken care of."

I had never met this man before and we had been in his office only an hour. Yet, all of this was happening! My wife and I went to the car and wondered, what had just happened. We repeated what had been said, and we both had heard the same thing. I called the person whom the businessman had told me to call, and the ball started rolling for my trip to Africa. I know I was thinking, "Why would I go to Africa now?"

But my wife assured me it was our Heavenly Father YAHUAH working. Other people told me our Heavenly Father YAHUAH had a purpose for my going. Our Heavenly Father YAHUAH had someone call us and tell us that YAHUAH had directed him to pay our bills. So, we knew YAHUAH wanted me to go to Africa.

Four months later, I was in Africa. I went to Kenya, Ethiopia, Uganda, and Tanzania. YAHUAH certainly does give us the desires of our hearts. I had a childhood desire to go to Africa and help build something to help the people there, and that is exactly what I did. I helped lay the foundation for a grinding mill for the women of the

Karapokot people in Northwest Kenya. As we were flying from Nairobi Kenya, I looked out the window and said to myself, "Africa is so beautiful. YAHUAH, why am I here?"

Our Heavenly Father YAHUAH spoke to my heart, "Enjoy my son, enjoy." Our Heavenly Father YAHUAH loves to bless His children with good gifts.

May He grant you according to your heart's desire,
And fulfill all your purpose.
Psalm 20:4 NKJV

One thing I have learned is that when YAHUAH blesses you, satan likes to come in and cause confusion. I say that because I don't want you to think for a moment that there were not obstacles put in my path. There were times when it looked as though I was not going to be able to go to Africa. My wife and I prayed, and we knew it was our Heavenly Father YAHUAH's will for me to go. This is when you have to have faith in YAHUAH.

The devil wants you to let go of your faith. Don't do it. If YAHUAH said it, He will complete it. YAHUAH is faithful.

My wife told me that while I was in Africa, she felt safe because she saw in The RUACH this very big angel outside of our house. It was standing guard over her and the kids and a heavenly peace came over her. She said she had never felt this way before, and I have traveled a lot. Our Heavenly Father YAHUAH continually gave us confirmation that it was His will for me to make the trip to Africa.

When I returned home, we continued to meet with people about sponsorship for the television show. Miraculous things continued to happen. We would go into meetings to talk with people about sponsorship, but instead of talking about sponsorship, they would talk about their personal lives. We knew we were there to listen. Our Heavenly Father YAHUAH would give us the answers to what they were looking for, and it would be confirmation to them. The people were always happy that we had spent time with them.

But we said, "YAHUAH, this is not working out the way we thought." We were going to meetings for business, but we ended up listening to people's problems and giving them answers.

We just wanted our Heavenly Father YAHUAH to know that we thought we were going to meetings to get sponsorship for the television show. After all, by getting these sponsorships, we could produce the television show and take care of our family. I didn't recognize it at the time, but our Heavenly Father YAHUAH was taking care of us. While I was doing what our Heavenly Father YAHUAH wanted me to, He was taking care of our family through other people.

People would call and tell us our Heavenly Father YAHUAH had told them to pay our bills. Everything was being taken care of, but it wasn't me doing it. This is when I learned that YAHUAH is the provider, and all I do is manage what He gives me.

We would go to meetings and people would say, "I don't really care about sponsoring your television show, but I do want to bless you personally."

I thought, "What was going on."

All this time I had never heard anybody, talk about this kind of provision from YAHUAH. I thought, "YAHUAH, do I have a lot to learn from you!" Now that I knew I was working for our Heavenly Father YAHUAH, I relaxed in the meetings and my mind was on what our Heavenly Father YAHUAH wanted to happen in the meeting. My wife and I had said we wanted to go higher with Him, so we asked our Heavenly Father YAHUAH what He wanted us to do, and our Heavenly Father YAHUAH was answering.

Our Heavenly Father YAHUAH was providing so much for us in so many different ways. We started to listen to some of the pastors on television talk shows about our Heavenly Father YAHUAH's provision. We knew we were experiencing provision from our Heavenly Father YAHUAH. We were beginning to hear about sowing and reaping on television and our pastor at our place of worship was also talking about sowing and reaping. We started to research our Bible on the subject. We learned that YAHUAH said in Romans 13:8 that we should owe no man anything, but love instead.

We thought, "Where did that come from?"

We had assumed we would always be in debt. It was the way things were supposed to be, wasn't it? We continued to read our Bible. One day we heard a pastor say you sow your way out of debt.

We thought, "How do you do that?"

The pastor had said that if you do not have all you need for your provision, take what you have, sow it into good ground, and believe YAHUAH for your return. We felt led to do just that, and we did. We were led to sow into four different ministries and believe for our return. We needed twenty thousand dollars to pay off all our bills. We wrote our checks out in our checkbook for the full amount of money for each bill and prayed over our checkbook. We left the checks in our checkbook and expected our return. We had heard all the pastors say you have to continue to thank YAHUAH for your return, so we did.

Every day I would say, "YAHUAH, I thank you that we are debt free, and we thank you for the increase, in YAHUSHA's name."

We had childlike faith. YAHUAH had us out there with Him now, and we trusted Him with all of our hearts.

During this time YAHUAH also instructed my wife to sow her wedding ring to my daughter. I said, "Are you sure He would want you to do this?"

But every time I looked at that ring, it shone and sparkled like never before, and I felt it was saying, "Give me away."

Then one day a minister appeared on television and said YAHUAH will not bless you past your last act of disobedience. I said to my wife, "Let's give her the ring now."

Our Heavenly Father YAHAUAH was sowing all kinds of things. He instructed my wife to call a woman who worked on the television show with her and tell her to come take any clothes she wanted. My wife took hand loads of clothing out of her closet. Some items still had tags on them. Then Andrea let the woman take her pick of the clothing, and she left our house very happy. My wife was then instructed by YAHUAH to take clothing and jewelry to our place of worship and give it away. One of the pieces of jewelry my wife gave to a woman was part of a matching set! We continued to give away whatever our Heavenly Father YAHUAH told us to give. It was so much fun to watch the reactions of people and to see people excited because of what YAHUAH was doing for them.

It was at this time that Andrea had a vision of an ax head flying through the air. We didn't know what the vision meant, so we started to ask people if they knew. Someone thought she had eaten too much pizza, and others didn't know what it meant.

Later, as we were watching a minster on television, he spoke about a story in the Bible about an ax head, in 2 Kings 6:5-7. We knew then that it hadn't been too much pizza. The vision had been about provision for debt, and about a meeting we were to attend the following week.

Our meeting was set up to talk about sponsorship for the television show. Again, the man we spoke with was not interested in the show, but he told us he would give us twenty thousand dollars! We were in shock, to say the least. We just sat there.

He continued to talk about what he was doing and about personal matters. We kept listening. At the end of the meeting, as we were getting ready to leave, we asked about the twenty thousand dollars. He asked us, "when do you want it?"

We said, "Now."

The man had his secretary make a check out to us right away for twenty thousand dollars. We had not been in that meeting more than an hour, and we left with a check for twenty thousand dollars. My dad had given us a ride to the meeting. When he picked us up, we showed him the check and told him how good it was to work for YAHUAH.

Our Heavenly Father YAHUAH will tell you to do something that just does not seem reasonable to your mind. I could not begin to tell you with words how good it is to trust YAHUAH as your provider. I thought I was a good provider. Our Heavenly Father YAHUAH is an awesome provider.

This was the manifestation of the vision of the ax head, the manifestation of doing what Our Heavenly Father YAHUAH instructed us to do.

We paid off all of our bills in full, and I was able to get my wife a bigger wedding ring than she had had before. Five years earlier, I had picked out that particular wedding ring for her. Now our Heavenly Father YAHUAH had me go and buy the ring for her-debt free, of course!

If you are willing and obedient,
You shall eat the good of the land.
Isaiah 1:19 NKJV

Chapter Three

~ ~ ~ ~ ~ ~ ~ ~ ~ ~

Andrea's Journey

Our Heavenly Father YAHUAH started to get me up at four o'clock in the morning to cook dinner. Then He would instruct me to call several people and ask them to come over to our house at the end of their workday to pray, and I would have dinner ready for them. We started to have prayer meetings in our house in the evenings, as our Heavenly Father YAHUAH instructed. We didn't have to know why our Heavenly Father YAHUAH wanted us to meet and pray. We just trusted His leading, and He moved mightily in all of our lives.

Our Heavenly Father YAHUAH started giving Melvin and me specific places to go. He would tell us the baby would fall asleep at a certain time, and the baby would fall asleep just when our Heavenly Father YAHUAH had said he would. We would go wherever our Heavenly Father YAHUAH told us to go.

Our Heavenly Father YAHUAH started directing us to go to another city and telling us we were going to live there.

He would have us pray for the city and the people there. He would send us there several times during the week to pray. Every time we would go there, I would be happy. But every time I would leave "our new" city after we prayed, I would feel sad. Melvin didn't know what to think about what was going on with me. He was happy with the house and the area we currently lived in. I had heard a lady say that when she left a particular area, she felt as though she left her heart. And that was exactly the way I felt.

I was in love with the people in the city YAHUAH had us praying for and moving to.

YAHUAH continued to lead us to different places, with the most interesting results. For example, once we were led to go to a car lot to look at cars. We ended up talking with a car salesman who just happened to be looking for a new assembly, and my husband just so happened to be the person who had recruited him into the military. When I say it "just happened," I'm kidding. It was all YAHUAH guiding and directing us.

That car salesman started to come to our assembly, and he loved it.

Something similar happened at another dealership. When we went there and began to talk with the salesman, we told him how far we drove to assembly. He got a revelation to look for a "good" place of worship, not just an assembly close to where he lived.

One day our Heavenly Father YAHUAH told us the airplane Melvin wanted was at a particular airport, so we went there and asked about the airplane. The people said they didn't have an airplane there, but they told us to come back and talk with someone the next day. When we went back the next day, the airplane was there in a hangar, and the salesperson let us see it. Our Heavenly Father YAHUAH was showing us just how much we were being led by Him, and that we knew His voice.

All the while, YAHUAH was also directing us as we contemplated moving into a new house.

When we looked for furniture and other furnishings, our Heavenly Father YAHUAH taught us how to select the best of everything. He was increasing us in every way. Our taste was changing in every area of our lives. He was teaching us to believe for His best. At the same time, He was sending us places, He continued to have us sowing things, giving things away, letting things go, and telling us to trust Him.

I cannot sufficiently convey to you how our Heavenly Father YAHUAH was continuing to let us know how to hear His voice and follow His direction. We could not doubt Him or His voice because of the way He was taking the direction of our lives. Melvin had been a private pilot but had given up flying. He had also given up his career in the military. I had given up my consultant business to go the direction of our Heavenly Father YAHUAH. We were giving so much of our personal things away. Everything had changed for us. Our plans were not our own anymore. We gave control of our plans to our Heavenly Father YAHUAH for His plans. Even though we knew this was our Heavenly Father YAHUAH's direction, we sometimes asked, "YAHUAH, are you sure this is what you want us to do?" He would always confirm, "Yes."

O YAHUAH, I know the way of man is not in himself;
it is not in man who walks to direct his own steps.
Jeremiah 10:23 NKJV

Melvin and I had always wanted to renew our marriage vows. One day our Heavenly Father YAHUAH impressed upon me to go to a particular bridal shop.

I went into the shop and there was a big sale. I started to look at all the beautiful dresses. I found a dress I loved and tried it on, thinking I would come back later when it was time for our vows to be renewed, and find a dress again. But when I tried on this dress, I could not believe the feeling that came over me. I felt like crying, I was overwhelmed with all kinds of emotions. I knew this was the dress I wanted. I hadn't thought I would wear a wedding dress when we renewed our vows. I had planned to wear an evening gown or something along that line. But this dress changed my mind about what I wanted to wear. I took the gown up to the desk and asked them to hold it for me. I had to find out how our Heavenly Father YAHUAH wanted to pay for it, because I didn't have enough money.

I went home and had a little talk with our Heavenly Father about the dress. I was not trying to buy anything at this time, but He obviously wanted me to have it now. YAHUAH gave me direction on what to do, and I followed His direction. The store put the dress on hold for me with the money I had available. A couple of months later, it was time to pay for the dress in full and I didn't have all the money. Melvin said he was going to get back the money we had put down on the dress. I sat in the car and told our Heavenly Father YAHUAH, "This was your idea to get this dress, not mine. Now I like it and I want it, so I want You to get it for me."

Melvin came out of the store and said we could pick the dress up at a later date. Our Heavenly Father YAHUAH was just teaching me to trust Him. He could have given me the money at that time, but He wanted me to trust Him.

Our Heavenly Father YAHUAH had provided for us so many times before that I knew He wasn't short on money or lacking in any way.

In case you are wondering how I could talk to our Heavenly Father YAHUAH that way, He said in the Bible, "Come boldly to the throne and let your request be known." (Hebrew 4:16) By now you probably know our Heavenly Father YAHUAH not only provided the money for the dress, but He provided over and above what we needed.

A few weeks later we were sitting in the kitchen and Melvin looked at me and said, "Let's go to the mall."

I didn't blink an eye. I said, "Let's go."

Melvin was not in the habit of saying, "Let's go to the mall," so I knew it was our Heavenly Father YAHUAH working. Then Melvin said, "Let's take the kids."

We found shoes on sale for the boys, and other things the kids needed. Melvin went into a jewelry store to look at wedding rings. Now, Melvin had started to look at wedding rings for himself, for when we would renew our vows, but he wasn't thinking about buying anything soon. However, when he was in this store, he found a ring he had been looking at in another store. The salesman quoted a price to him that was half the price he had been quoted at the other store. Melvin talked to the manager.

The manager told Melvin the salesperson had misquoted the price fifty percent, so he had to give Melvin that price but Melvin had to purchase the ring that day. Melvin told the manager he didn't have the money with him but he could give him one hundred dollars to hold the price. The manager agreed. We left the mall and went home. Melvin then called the jeweler at the store where he had first seen the ring. That jeweler told Melvin he couldn't get a better deal, and that he should purchase the other ring, so Melvin went back and purchased the second ring. Our Heavenly

Father YAHUAH was telling us to do things we would not otherwise have thought about doing at this time in our lives.

Our Heavenly Father YAHUAH's timing was certainly different from ours. We would purchase everything when our Heavenly Father YAHUAH said to purchase it, even clothes.

I had been looking in the mall for weeks before our Heavenly Father YAHUAH finally impressed upon me to go to the mall to buy a shirt I wanted. Then when I got there, the shirt was on sale and there was only one shirt left in my size, and it was stuck between other garments. Now I could see that our Heavenly Father YAHUAH saves things just for us. This was so awesome! He had blessed me with clothes before, but this was different. I knew He had saved this particular shirt just for me.

Another time, YAHUAH impressed upon me to go to a shoe store I really liked. YAHUAH told me to purchase shoes for all the times Melvin had not bought anything for me when he had been working out of town so much. I know YAHUAH's voice and I knew this was Him, so I purchased five pairs of shoes with a credit card. I was a little nervous because I didn't know how Melvin would react.

But he knew I hadn't done anything like this before. To purchase with a credit card didn't seem right to me, but I knew this was our Heavenly Father YAHUAH speaking, so I did it. And you know what happened. YAHUAH provided all the money to pay off the credit card bill. YAHUAH is such a good provider!

Our Heavenly Father YAHUAH started providing in such a way that every time I would go to the store, things would be on sale even if I didn't see a sale sign on them. By the time I would get to the counter, it would be on sale! One day I was watching television and the minister was talking about the favor of YAHUAH. I realized that was what was going on with me on a regular basis now. Not just now and then, but all the time!

Our Heavenly Father YAHUAH had begun to talk with us more about moving, so we started looking more in the area YAHUAH had impressed on us to move to.

I had begun to get a vision, but it was not a vision of where I thought we were supposed to move at this time. We started to follow the instruction we were getting from our

Heavenly Father YAHUAH, but it wasn't what I had expected.

During this time a friend of ours was in town and she stayed with us. Our Heavenly Father YAHUAH began to confirm through our friend everything that was going on. She told us we were doing what our Heavenly Father YAHUAH wanted us to do and moving in the direction He wanted us to go.

We thought we were moving to the city we had been praying for but ended up staying with my brother instead. My vision had been of my brother's house, but I thought this could not be so. Our Heavenly Father YAHUAH had us praying for a certain area, and in love with those people. What was going on now?

We simply followed the direction our Heavenly Father YAHUAH gave us. YAHUAH had been preparing us to move for a long time. We had been giving things away, talking about what to do with the house, and so forth. We were prepared to move, but not in the direction we were going.

I had a vision of my brother's house, and another vision of the place to get a moving truck for the belongings we had left. I told Melvin the name of the moving company I had seen in the vision. He went to another moving company, and they didn't have a truck. When Melvin went to the business I had seen in the vision, there was one truck available in the size we needed. We talked with my brother, and he told us we could come to his house. At the time, we did not understand what was going on, but we knew this was what our Heavenly Father YAHUAH wanted us to do. He confirmed it with a word from a minister on television.

He said this was a setup for one of the biggest miracles and one of the biggest testimonies we had ever seen. This is the scripture we were given:

And we know that all things work together for good to those who love YAHUAH, to those who are the called according to His purpose.
Romans 8:28 NKJV

Our Heavenly Father YAHUAH spoke to Melvin and me, saying, "You have more now than most people in this world." We said, "If you say so, YAHUAH." Our Heavenly Father YAHUAH let us know He was with us and we were going to have a wonderful time in YAHUAH. Our Heavenly Father YAHUAH does not require this lifestyle of everyone, but He required it of us. There were other people who said they wanted to quit their jobs and be with our Heavenly Father YAHUAH, but we told them they had better stay where our Heavenly Father YAHUAH had them. They could see the peace and joy we had in YAHUAH and His hand on our lives. We knew how to make money and buy houses; material things were always easy for us to come by. We knew we could get jobs anytime we wanted to if we wanted to be out of the will of our Heavenly Father YAHUAH.

At about that time, our pastor delivered a sermon explaining that sometimes our Heavenly Father YAHUAH will take you on a path so far away from what He had told you, you will think that you have not heard from Him at all. This sermon really helped us, because His path was looking very different from the way we had envisioned it.

Every time we were not sure of something, our Heavenly Father YAHUAH kept giving us a Word from someone, usually a pastor at our place of worship or on television, to confirm we were on the right path.

So YAHUSHA answered and said, "Assuredly, I say to you, there is no one who has left house or brothers or sisters or father or mother or wife or children or lands, for

My sake and the gospel's who shall not receive a hundredfold now in this time—houses and brothers and sisters and mothers and children and lands, with

persecutions—and in the age to come, eternal life."
Mark 10:29,30 NKJV

We experienced the persecutions of people thinking we were crazy for leaving all we had. Our lives changed so much. We were the people who had always had material things. And we knew we would have them again, but with a different mindset. We understood that our Heavenly Father YAHUAH was our source now, and everything we had belonged to Him. Something wonderful was happening to us. A new anointing was present in our everyday lives. The anointing was strong, like that we had previously experienced when we were at our place of worship praying with a pastor.

Materially, there was little for us to be happy about, yet we had a deep peace. And we felt the presence of YAHUAH as though we were in a corporate anointing in our place of worship. We realized that we had divine peace from our Heavenly Father YAHUAH. We loved the peace, but we also wanted people to understand what was happening with us.

We discovered that our Heavenly Father YAHUAH did not want us to care about man's opinion of us, only that we pleased Him. And He said He was well pleased with us. This was not a call to poverty (just in case anyone would try to read that into this.) No way! We continued to learn YAHUAH's way of increasing us in every area of our lives.

We discovered that people tend to judge others by what they have and not by their character. We had always known this, but now we were experiencing it firsthand. We could also see that not many people cared how much we loved our Heavenly Father YAHUAH or how much love we had for each other. And I am not talking about unbelievers. I am talking about believers who should know you by The RUACH and by your fruit rather than by your material possessions. We know many people who have material things but got them the wrong way. We could have gotten jobs and replaced everything we had before, but we would have missed out on what our Heavenly Father YAHUAH was showing us. We learned so much about people, and we could not believe what we were learning. Or, perhaps I should say we did not want to believe what we were learning. It was hard to experience how shallow many people were and what they really believed in their hearts. our Heavenly Father YAHUAH deliberately sent us certain people so we could see their true hearts.

Our Heavenly Father YAHUAH began to have us pray for people. We had a schedule for praying for people as though it were a regular job. There were a lot of hurting people around us who needed someone to just listen and pray.

We were at an assembly camp meeting when YAHUAH instructed Melvin to talk to this particular man he knew about some T-Shirts Melvin wanted from the camp meeting. So, Melvin spoke to him. The man told Melvin, "YAHUAH has been talking to me about blessing you with T-shirts, but I thought I might offend you, so I didn't do it." They laughed about it because the man was being prideful. Melvin also had a hard time talking with him about it, but they finally got around to doing what our Heavenly Father YAHUAH wanted. After the man blessed Melvin with the money for the T-shirts, someone came along right behind Melvin and blessed that man. Our Heavenly Father YAHUAH had been trying to get the man to bless Melvin so He could bless the man.

We were learning more and more about sowing and reaping. We were waiting for our income tax check so we could get some tapes and other things from the assembly camp meeting. Our Heavenly Father YAHUAH directed us to get our eyes off the income tax check and on Him instead. We did as our Heavenly Father YAHUAH instructed, and then someone else blessed us with the tapes we wanted. Our Heavenly Father YAHUAH wanted us to know He was still the provider. For example, when we received our income tax return check, we had extra money because YAHUAH had already provided us with the things we had intended to buy with that check. Our Heavenly Father YAHUAH gave us the following scripture:

Now to Him who is able to do exceedingly abundantly above all that we ask or think, according to the power that works in us.
Ephesians 3:20 NKJV

We purchased a book from one of the ministers in the meeting. He signed the book and quoted Ephesians 3:20. Our Heavenly Father YAHUAH always confirmed what He was telling us, and we needed a lot of confirmation at that time. Another minister in the meeting told a story that sounded like what had happened to us, and our Heavenly

Father YAHUAH had done something similar with his life. Our Heavenly Father YAHUAH kept letting us know we were not alone or crazy.

The minister told us he had been ministering in big assemblies, staying in the big hotels, and making a good living, when our Heavenly Father YAHUAH told him to pack up his desk. Our Heavenly Father YAHUAH did not tell him where he was going, but the minister went from fine hotels to living with people and sleeping on cots.

Our Heavenly Father YAHUAH was determined we were going to do things His way. Melvin tried to sell his motorcycle, and he put it outside in front of my brother's house with a "For Sale" sign on it. For several days, my brother would bring the sign back from down the street. The sign had blown off of the motorcycle even when there was no wind. After so many days of this, a friend told us, "Just take the sign off of the bike. YAHUAH doesn't want you to sell it."

Our Heavenly Father YAHUAH continued to bless us every day. We would leave the house in the morning and on my way to a meeting or prayer assignment, I would stop by a gas station for coffee. When I would get to the counter, the clerk would tell me the coffee was free. I thought, "What a nice guy." Later that evening I went back to the gas station and the gas station attendant said, "It is free." But this was a different person! The next day I went to a totally different gas station and that attendant also said, "It is free." This went on for weeks. No matter what station we went to, I would get free coffee.

You may recall a friend of mine had gotten free clothing when she was with me. Well, she started going with me for coffee and, you guessed it, she started getting free coffee too. Melvin said to me, "If you get free coffee, I know I get free coffee." And he did. I watched to see if other people were also getting it, but they weren't. One day I put money on the counter for my coffee and the gas station attendant gave it back to me. And another time, I went to a gas station to get milk and the lady there paid for half of the milk. Favor was showing up all over the place. These, as you can see, were not isolated incidents. We were walking in the divine favor of YAHUAH.

We would pray at our place of worship on Monday night, Tuesday morning, Friday morning and at other times.

One time they had canceled prayer at our place of worship, but a few people showed up anyway. The RUACH HA'QODESH had instructed all of us to come, so the pastor gave us a room to pray in. Our Heavenly Father was telling us again, "You are led by Me."

We started to think about working more, but our Heavenly Father YAHUAH told us to fall forward on the written Word of YAHUAH, not on work. The work will come because you put the Word of YAHUAH first. Work was never a problem for us. We liked to work, but our Heavenly Father YAHUAH was trying to teach us order. The Word of YAHUAH should be directing our work along with the guidance of The RUACH HA'QODESH.

Our minds were being renewed to the Word of YAHUAH and YAHUAH's way of doing things, and the anointing continued to increase in our lives. As we would pray for people, they would get answers to their prayers.

We really wanted more money at that time, even though our Heavenly Father YAHUAH was providing. I said I would try to get a part-time job outside of the meetings for the television show, even though I wasn't sure whether our Heavenly Father YAHUAH agreed. Our minds were still being renewed to YAHUAH's way of doing things.

One night during the time I was considering returning to work, our Heavenly Father YAHUAH instructed me to go to our place of worship to listen to the pastor. During his sermon the pastor said if you get a job, even if it is to pay your rent and take care of your family, if it is not where our Heavenly Father YAHUAH told you to be, you would be just like a prostitute working for money. When I heard that, I jumped all over myself. I said to Melvin, "Did you hear that? He said I would be a prostitute!" By this time, Melvin had had enough of our Heavenly Father YAHUAH's spankings, so he wasn't trying to work outside of the television show. And I wasn't going to think about it anymore either. That was enough for me. My problem was not with YAHUAH; I was still concerned about what other people were thinking and trying to get the pressure off myself instead of praying and letting our Heavenly Father YAHUAH help me.

Chapter Four

~ ~ ~ ~ ~ ~ ~ ~ ~ ~

Sold Out For YAHUAH

Our Heavenly Father let us know this book we were writing, was about the path our Heavenly Father YAHUAH had us on. We thought it was about the television show, but the book ended up being much more than that.

One day our Heavenly Father YAHUAH instructed us to go to the airport. Melvin was happy. He had not been at the airport for quite some time, and being a pilot, he really wanted to go. When we arrived, there was an "Aviation Day," an open house to look at airplanes. Our Heavenly Father YAHUAH told me to pay attention to a particular Hispanic couple who were looking at an airplane. The couple began to talk with us, and we started to talk about our Heavenly Father YAHUAH. They were believers who were looking for a place to worship, and we ended up taking them to our place of worship. Our pastor had always said our place of worship would be an international assembly where everyone was welcome. Our guest loved the assembly. Whenever our Heavenly Father YAHUAH instructed us to do something, it was always about people who were looking for our Heavenly Father YAHUAH or a place of worship. In response, we were bringing increase to the assembly. One day our pastor told Melvin, "You are bringing a lot of people to our assembly."

We knew what increase was really about. It was about increasing the kingdom of YAHUAH.

And we understood that in turn, YAHUAH would increase us.

But seek first the kingdom of YAHUAH and His righteousness, and all these things shall be added to you. Matthew 6:33 NKJV

We were starting to accumulate some bills, so we asked our Heavenly Father YAHUAH what we should do about this. Our Heavenly Father YAHUAH told Melvin he needed to make a vow to Him. There was a pastor coming into town for a convention.

Our Heavenly Father YAHUAH had shown me a vision that Melvin and I were to attend the convention, so we did. I didn't know what making a vow really meant until the ministering pastor said, "If you need your bills paid, our Heavenly Father YAHUAH wants you to make a vow."

Then the pastor told us what to say and what to do. We put a rubber band around all of our bills and prayed over them. Then Melvin made a vow to our Heavenly Father YAHUAH that we would use our money as our Heavenly Father YAHUAH instructed him. Everything we had belonged to our Heavenly Father YAHUAH, not to us. During the next few days our Heavenly Father YAHUAH started talking with us about going out of town to attend a convention at the assembly of the pastor we had just seen. We thought, here we are, talking to our Heavenly Father YAHUAH about paying our bills, and He wants us to go out of town. We prayed, and YAHUAH gave me another vision to go on the trip.

We then asked, "Well, YAHUAH, what do you want us to do? We need some money. We need someone to keep the kids. We need a hotel room, airfare, a rental car, groceries, and clothing for the kids". YAHUAH was really stretching us big time.

YAHUAH kept us praying as the weeks went by. We kept waiting for provision for our trip. YAHUAH continued to lead us to pray for people. As we were praying for a particular lady and her business, I saw in The RUACH something that looked like a tornado, so we prayed for protection. The very next day there were straight-line winds so bad that they damaged all the businesses around hers, and many business owners had to close their doors. But her business, the only one untouched by the storm, was not damaged at all. Our Heavenly Father YAHUAH is indeed an awesome and good ELOHIYM!

We were blessed with the privilege of praying with so many people. The following are testimonies from a few of these people:

SOWING SEED AND THE POWER OF AGREEMENT:

We ended up bidding on four houses we liked, but we were unsuccessful in getting any of them. We were unsure of why this kept happening, so we prayed and asked YAHUAH for the answers.

My husband got a revelation about sowing seed in the Rhines' household, so we sowed a financial seed. On several occasions we prayed and came into agreement with Melvin and Andrea, believing we would have a home for our family, by faith. We believed our sown seed and prayer would be answered.

The prayer was answered with a house we love, by being obedient to The RUACH HA'QODESH and coming together and with the Rhineses. We believed and got our breakthrough. -Ed and Melanie Lacy

TAKE THE TIME TO PRAY FOR HURTING PEOPLE AROUND YOU:

One day in our place of worship, Melvin looked at me and recognized the pain in my eyes and how nervous and upset I was. After the service Melvin and Andrea asked us if we were going to get together to pray about my move out of town. We set up a meeting to pray. For our prayer session we got together at the home of my daughter, son-in law, and grandson. WOW! What a night. I got my answer. After that night I couldn't believe how much pressure had been on me. What a relief in my mind, body, and soul. I was able to continue doing my job without the pain of not knowing what to do. It was as though nothing had ever burdened me. My wife and I had continued to move in the direction we should be going, toward YAHUAH and YAHUSHA HA'MASHIACH the Almighty. -Larry and Karen Klein

BE WILLING TO BE INTERRUPTED FOR YAHUAH AND HIS PURPOSE:

My testimony is that Andrea came over to visit me for one reason, but YAHUAH had His own plan. YAHUAH had led us to go to my friend's house. The RUACH YAHUAH moved, and Andrea led everyone to pray as a group. Through her YAHUAH ministered, and all that was ministered through her that day came to pass. The RUACH YAHUAH fell, yokes were broken, and depression was lifted. Children whom satan was trying to snatch away were restored. Since that day, one young woman has changed her heart and mind, and she is now headed to a more mature relationship with our Heavenly Father YAHUAH. There were five of us there that day. YAHUAH not only sent Andrea that day, but He also ministered through her. YAHUAH's Word is the same today, yesterday, tomorrow, and forevermore. What our Heavenly Father YAHUAH says He will do, He will do. -Sherree Ellis

AN OPPORTUNITY TO LEAD SOMEONE TO THE MASHIACH:

I was feeling very stressed out and had a severe headache because I was going through a terrible situation. Melvin and Andrea called me, and I shared with them how I was feeling. They offered to pray with me. We prayed about my situation, and then we prayed and I surrendered my life to YAHUSHA HA'MASHIACH. By the time the prayer was over, my headache was gone. -Thomas

AN OPPORTUNITY TO LEAD SOMEONE BACK TO MASHIACH:

I had been a born-again, RUACH-filled believer for twenty years, and I have been in ministry most of that time. But in the last year, attacks and trials came into my life so powerfully that I was eventually overtaken by discouragement, disappointment, frustration, and depression. I felt that YAHUAH was not there for me, or for the whole assembly body, for that matter.

I began to run in the direction of sin. I was in a bar one night and met a man. I began to see him. We were in a restaurant late one evening when Melvin and Andrea came in. They sat with us because they knew the man I was with. In the middle of the conversation, we started to talk about my life.

I had a second to contemplate whether I should lie or bare all. It was midnight and our Heavenly Father YAHUAH had sent Andrea and Melvin into this restaurant.

They began to talk to me and even pray for us right there in the restaurant. I felt a softening of my heart. I realized that I had a bad attitude towards YAHUAH, and I admitted it. They ministered to me, saying "YAHUSHA loves you, even if you have fallen away." It hit me like a wave, and I started to cry. I went to place of worship with Melvin and Andrea the next morning, and Andrea led me to the altar to rededicate myself to our Heavenly Father YAHUAH. That statement that YAHUSHA loves me even if I have fallen away still rings clear in my heart. -Pam

Chapter Five

~ ~ ~ ~ ~ ~ ~ ~ ~ ~

Traveling Deeper

Back talking about our life in YAHUAH, Melvin and I had been very busy praying for people and taking care of our children. We were still waiting for our Heavenly Father YAHUAH to give us instructions about the trip to the out-of-town convention. I told our Heavenly Father YAHUAH, "I need you to answer me by tonight at the service. If I don't hear your answer, I guess we are not to go."

At the end of the assembly service, our Heavenly Father YAHUAH directed me to tell a particular couple we knew about our situation. YAHUAH told me to tell them the amount of money we needed and ask them to pray a prayer of agreement. We did, and they prayed with us for thirteen hundred dollars. After we prayed, they told us Our Heavenly Father YAHUAH had been dealing with them earlier to give us some money and they knew this was the time to do so. They wrote us a check, but we still needed more, so we kept praying for direction from our Heavenly Father. We needed to leave the next day. During this time, a lady told us she believed our Heavenly Father YAHUAH had called us, but we were on the wrong track. I was troubled by this, so I called a friend of mine. I also talked to another friend about the situation. Our Heavenly Father had both of these women praying for us. He also had used them to speak into our lives. They both said, "Do not pay attention to what was said to you but keep doing what our Heavenly Father YAHUAH told you to do. Do not listen to the lies of the devil."

We were so happy we hadn't listened to the devil. The lady did not know she was doing anything wrong. The devil was just using her to try to stop us from going on this trip. Melvin talked with my mother, and she said she would keep the children. The next morning people started bringing money to our house. Melvin's dad provided the clothing we wanted for the kids. We received all the money we needed, thirteen hundred dollars. Melvin was able to cash at one bank all the checks people had given us, and we bought groceries to make sure the kids and my mom would have everything they would need while we were gone.

Next, we went to a clothing store and bought traveling clothes for ourselves and clothes for our sons. We left for the airport that same afternoon. We accomplished all of that in one afternoon.

Let me explain why I added that they let Melvin cash all the checks at one bank. For one thing, it was not our bank! And not only did we not have an account there, but the checks were also from different banks. Banks don't normally do that. Our Heavenly Father YAHUAH moved on the hearts of people for that to happen. The way had been prepared. All we had to do was follow the leading of our Heavenly Father YAHUAH. We called just before we left home and we were able to get a hotel room and rent a car. Everything we asked our Heavenly Father YAHUAH for, He gave us. You know it took faith to hold on to what I knew our Heavenly Father YAHUAH had told me, even when it didn't happen in the timing, I thought it should happen. Our Heavenly Father YAHUAH had His perfect timing. Sometimes if we are not receiving from our Heavenly Father YAHUAH, it is because we have a timetable, and we want our Heavenly Father YAHUAH to provide for us our way and in our timing. But our Heavenly Father YAHUAH has purpose in everything He does.

One thing my husband and I learned was that our thinking was very shallow compared to our Heavenly Father

YAHUAH's plan for our life. YAHUAH is an awesome and good ELOHIYM.

And YAHUAH shall supply all your needs according to His riches in glory by MASHIACH YAHUSHA. Philippians 4:19 NKJV

On our first day at the convention, we met a pastor and his wife. Our Heavenly Father YAHUAH sat us in front of them, and we started to talk with them before the first session began. Our Heavenly Father YAHUAH directed us to ask them to go to lunch, and we ministered to them about their marriage. We were able to bless them with a tape about our Heavenly Father YAHUAH's path being different from our path, the same tape that had blessed us so much previously.

It really helped them decide to stay exactly where our Heavenly Father YAHUAH had them, in ministry. It was amazing to see our Heavenly Father YAHUAH work in their lives. Our Heavenly Father YAHUAH is so faithful. We ministered to them through the week of the conference.

During that week, Melvin had a desire to receive the gift of tongues. He was told by one of the ministers to come and just be in corporate prayer every day, so we did. He also ministered to Melvin with compassion, and he assured Melvin had not done anything wrong that was blocking his ability to receive tongues. When we started going to corporate prayer before the services, the devil tried to offend Melvin in all kinds of ways.

We recognized what was going on, and we stayed in peace. The next morning in our hotel, Melvin awakened to the floodgates of The RUACH HA'QODESH with the evidence of speaking in tongues. What a glorious time we had! I felt a pressure or weight lift off of me, as though I had been carrying something. Melvin was so excited; all he had to do was relax. Our getting away and out of town had helped him.

We headed back to the conference, and the Word of YAHUAH was going forth with such power. One of the ministers called pastors to the front in order to lay hands on them to prosper. Before I knew it, I was pushing Melvin out of his seat. Up to the front we went to get ministered to. When the minister laid hands on us, we started speaking in tongues. We fell to the floor, and we knew we had received an impartation. When we returned to our seats, I saw an angel come down in front of me. Melvin asked me, "Are you seeing something?" I asked him, "Why are you asking me if I am seeing something?" He didn't seem to know why he was asking because he didn't see anything. I told him, "Yes, I am seeing an angel," and he didn't seem surprised. He would ask me now and then if the angel was still there and I would tell him yes.

I told you earlier that we had put a rubber band around all of our bills and Melvin had made a vow to our Heavenly Father YAHUAH. Well, all of a sudden, I saw the rubber band bursting off of the bills and all the bills flying away into the air! Now I saw this in The RUACH.

Then all kinds of things started to happen. A year before we went to this conference, our Heavenly Father YAHUAH had told Melvin and me a double-portion blessing was going to come to us. The next day in the service, an urge to run came over me. I had never felt this feeling before. A few minutes later, a calm feeling came over me. I sat in my seat in a calmness I had never felt before. All of a sudden, the minister started to tell how our Heavenly Father YAHUAH had given him instructions to do something, and our Heavenly Father YAHUAH told him he would receive a double portion.

The minister started to run. Then another minister started to run, and then I started to run. I ran all over my husband and others trying to get out of my seat. I ran around the entire dome along with two other ministers, making a noise that sounded like a foghorn. When I got back to my seat, I was not tired even though I was wearing a dress and high heel shoes! When I returned to my seat, my husband looked at me, wondering what had happened to me. Of course I did not know, but it felt wonderful, and I was certainly excited and full of joy.

Melvin and I knew we were changing. Every day we were so full of The RUACH HA'QODESH. We were in such complete awe of our Heavenly Father YAHUAH. We were so thankful we hadn't listened to the lady who had told us we were on the wrong road. Our Heavenly Father YAHUAH instructed Melvin to take money to the altar at the front of the assembly, and to take one hundred dollars to the pastor we had ministered to that week. Melvin took the one hundred dollars and put it in one of the pastor's pockets. Melvin told him our Heavenly Father YAHUAH had said it was for him and not his ministry. When Melvin returned to his seat, our Heavenly Father YAHUAH instructed Melvin to go back to the pastor again, take another one hundred dollars, and tell the pastor it was for his other pocket. And when Melvin did this, that pastor was so blessed that he just started to cry. He was so thankful to our Heavenly Father YAHUAH.

Our Heavenly Father YAHUAH was letting that pastor know He would take care of his every need. He needed to go back and trust our Heavenly Father YAHUAH in his ministry. He was to live by faith, not by sight. He was encouraged and was able to leave and be determined to do what our Heavenly Father YAHUAH wanted him to do.

When we were getting ready to leave the assembly that night, something very strange happened. First of all, the angel was still standing in front of me. Most of the people had left the assembly, but a few of us were still there. All of a sudden, there were people underneath our seats, praying in The RUACH. The security people stood at the end of our row and did not let anyone down the row, and neither Melvin nor I could move. We felt stuck in our seats as they continued to pray for quite a while. When they stopped, we were able to leave the assembly and the angel left with us. We went to our rooms to pack and we left the next morning. When we got to the airport, the angel was still with us. The angel was so close to me that it was as though the angel was connected to my side. I was not frightened. I felt safe, and it was kind of funny to me. I thought, "We have a prosperity angel," because that is how I felt. I told Melvin, "We have a prosperity angel." I just knew that was what we had. The angel stayed with us in the airport until we got on the plane. Then I couldn't see the angel anymore, but I knew the angel was still there, with us forever.

I felt strengthened and comforted. We were no longer the same. When we returned home, our Heavenly Father YAHAUH instructed us to test the anointing, so Melvin called a friend of ours who worked at a BMW car dealership. They got into a BMW on the show floor and Melvin prayed for him to prosper. That same afternoon, the friend called Melvin and said his manager wanted to know what had happened to him because he had sold four cars in a matter of a few hours. He told Melvin whatever he did to him worked. Melvin's friend was out of breath and in awe of what had happened. Glory to YAHUAH! What an awesome ELOHIYM!

We had sown so much financial seed while we were away that we didn't have enough money to cover all our expenses upon our return home. But as you might guess. Our Heavenly Father YAHUAH moved on the heart of another person to sow seed into us.

Again, we had all the daily provision we needed. Still, I was believing YAHUAH was going to pay off all of our bills, so every day I thanked our Heavenly Father YAHUAH for paying off all our bills, and sometimes I did this more than once a day! We had made payments on our bills, but I told our Heavenly Father YAHUAH I didn't have payment faith, I had debt-free faith. I continued to thank our Heavenly Father YAHUAH for all our bills being paid. One day a friend of ours called and told us our Heavenly Father YAHUAH wanted him to seed money to us, so we went to pray with him. Our friend had told us an amount on the phone, but when we got there, he told us our Heavenly Father YAHUAH had told him to double the amount. A few days went by and our Heavenly Father YAHUAH instructed us to go pray with our friend again. We found out he had a breakthrough in his business. A deal he had been working on for a long time had come through. Then our Heavenly Father YAHUAH instructed him to sow a seed of ten thousand dollars to us. We paid our tithes, sowed seed money into other people, paid off all of our bills, and took our sons on vacation. Our Heavenly Father YAHUAH is so faithful.

We wanted a van to take our vacation in. A friend called us and told us our Heavenly Father YAHUAH wanted her to rent a van for us. All these wonderful things kept happening to us. But when we went to rent the van, the clerk told the lady her credit card limit had already been reached. We started to leave, but all of a sudden, the anointing of our Heavenly Father YAHUAH hit me and YAHUAH said, "There is favor all around you." We went to another car rental business and as it turned out, our friend rented the van for not one, but two weeks. The business renewed the car rental for an additional week upon our return! The favor of YAHUAH is miraculous. If YAHUAH is for you, who can be against you?

When we reached our vacation destination, we had not called ahead for hotel reservations. We just wanted our Heavenly Father YAHUAH to direct us to the place we had already told Him we wanted. Again, He did exactly that. Our Heavenly Father YAHUAH instructed us to go down a certain street, and there was the hotel with a vacancy. The hotel had everything we had asked our Heavenly Father YAHUAH for.

We had a wonderful vacation. Glory to YAHUAH!

Upon our return home from vacation, we stayed with my mom for a short time. I told our Heavenly Father YAHUAH that if it was not time for our home, I would like a place of our own again.

Then our Heavenly Father YAHUAH did exactly as I had requested of Him. He moved us into a fully furnished place with everything we needed. It came complete with a swimming pool, and we even had people to clean for us! There were also very nice people around us. Our Heavenly Father YAHUAH spoke to me and said this was manifested Word. I had spoken this out of my mouth, and He brought it to pass. This had happened more than once before, but this was more than I could comprehend. Our Heavenly Father had said "manifested Word." This was not just YAHUAH's favor. I had something to do with this.

YAHUAH is gracious and full of compassion,
Slow to anger and great in mercy.
YAHUAH is good to all,
And His tender mercies are over all His works.
Psalm 145:8,9 NKJV

The young lions lack and suffer hunger; But those who see YAHUAH shall not lack any good thing.

Psalm 34:10 NKJV

For you, O YAHUAH, will bless the righteous;
With favor You will surround him as with a shield

Psalm 5:12 NKJV

Chapter Six

~ ~ ~ ~ ~ ~ ~ ~ ~

Changing From Glory To Glory

We had our own place again, and it felt good. What a relief. We were in the city where our Heavenly Father had told us we were going to move. Our Heavenly Father YAHUAH started to deal with Melvin about being led more by The RUACH. YAHUAH was taking him away from how he had been operating in the past. He started to lead Melvin more and more. YAHUAH would have Melvin go talk with the building manager, and he even told Melvin what to tell the manager. This was very uncomfortable for Melvin because sometimes we did not have rent money when we thought we should have it. However, our Heavenly Father YAHUAH would give Melvin detailed directions on what to tell the manager. Melvin just wanted to have the money, but our Heavenly Father YAHUAH was continuing to teach Melvin to be led and do things our Heavenly Father YAHUAH's way instead of Melvin's way. He was teaching Melvin to live by The RUACH and not by sight. Our Heavenly Father

YAHUAH continued to help Melvin with his carnal nature, but this was not easy.

Moving on with YAHUAH in our lives, one day Melvin and I went to a grocery store. Before we could get inside, a lady came over and started talking to us about her basket, which was full of juice. It was juice the store was replacing with a new product. She did not want to throw it away, so she asked us whether we wanted it. It had not expired, and nothing was wrong with it, so we accepted the juice and took it home. There was so much juice that we had to put it in the refrigerator, our cabinets, and extra storage places. What a provider YAHUAH is! Yes, our Heavenly Father YAHUAH is an awesome provider.

This life we were living was certainly different from the life we had known before YAHUAH was providing for us. It was so different from what we had previously experienced. Our Heavenly Father YAHUAH told us, "You do not know who you are," and He said, "You do not know how to be taken care of." We didn't think we were supposed to be taken care of. We were adults and we thought we were supposed to take care of ourselves. This new concept gave us head cramps. We asked our Heavenly

Father YAHUAH, "What do you mean, we don't know how to be taken care of?"

What we did understand was that from now on our Heavenly Father YAHUAH was going to be directing us in every area of our lives. Not just when we did not know what to do, but all the time. His plans were going to be our plans. We were supposed to take life one day at a time and not be concerned about the future. It was an ongoing adjustment that had to be drilled into our hearts and minds.

Therefore do not worry about tomorrow, for tomorrow will worry about its own things. Sufficient for the day is its own trouble.
Mathew 6:34 NKJV

We met a lot of wonderful people in our apartment complex. Some of the people were believers, some were not. But all of them had an impact on our lives, and we influenced our neighbors as well.

Day in and day out, our Heavenly Father YAHUAH continued to work, on the way we thought about things. He would tell us to go pray with certain people, and they would sow seed into us. In this way, our Heavenly Father

YAHUAH provided for us and we had enough money for our rent, food, and other items we needed.

Blessed be YAHUAH,
Who daily loads us with benefits,
The ELOHIYM of our salvation!
Psalm 68:19 NKJV

I have been young, and now am old;
Yet I have not seen the righteous forsaken,
Nor his descendants begging bread
Psalm 37:25 NKJV

Cast your burden on YAHUAH,
And He shall sustain you;
He shall never permit the righteous to be moved.
Psalm 55:22 NKJV

Our Heavenly Father YAHUAH talked to us about how He was sustaining us, and we were actually discounting His sustenance.

We wanted to work to acquire more sponsors for the television show, but YAHUAH wanted us available to pray for people and to study the Word.

We didn't really want to do things the way our Heavenly Father YAHUAH was telling us to do them, because we felt we were not doing enough. We thought we needed to work, work, work. But our Heavenly Father YAHUAH wanted our lives to be directed and not driven. We were very driven people. We prided ourselves on taking good care of ourselves and our family. But our Heavenly Father YAHUAH wanted us to learn to trust Him more, rather than trust our own thinking. YAHUAH wanted to talk with us during prayer, to give us instructions. And He wanted us to carry out His instructions, which were usually totally different from what we would have done on our own.

Chapter Seven

~ ~ ~ ~ ~ ~ ~ ~ ~ ~

Melvin's Revelation

Our Heavenly Father YAHUAH told me to have devotional time with our sons and with my wife. He was teaching me how to be the head of my family. He wanted me to be a covering for them, much more than just a provider.

I would take my sons to school. The rest of the time, I would spend in the Word of YAHUAH and praying. Our Heavenly Father YAHUAH gave me instructions on what we should do about the business, how to be a father to my sons and a husband to my wife. I thought I was doing a good job already, but I found out I had much to improve upon to achieve YAHUAH's best. I had to relearn how to be a father and a husband. But thank YAHUAH, His grace is sufficient for all of us.

I knew how to provide money for my family, but I had much to learn about being the head of our family and a covering. I had to learn how to pray over my family, our business, and for other people. Our Heavenly Father YAHUAH had me find scriptures for my family to confess over our lives every day, not just now and then. I had to learn more about being directed by The RUACH HA'QODESH in my prayer time. My prayer time, learning how to pray, and discovering how to confess scripture concerning my family really paid off.

One Summer day when my wife was out of town, my sons and I went canoeing. My two younger sons, four and seven at the time, were in the canoe with me. We were heading back to shore from having a great time when my four-year-old, who had been sitting between my legs, suddenly stood up in the canoe. It tipped over and we all fell overboard into the water. I saw my seven-year-old fly out of the canoe. I wasn't too concerned because they were wearing their life jackets, but I couldn't see them, and they should have been floating.

I made my way back to the canoe and I flipped it over. Both boys were sitting in the canoe, screaming! They weren't even spitting up water or choking. I know my sons were protected because of my prayers and the scriptures I confess over my family. I had seen my seven-year-old fly out of the canoe. In the natural, he wouldn't have been in the canoe when I tipped it back upright. You would have thought my boys should at least be coughing. Thank you, YAHUAH, for Your protection and guidance!

What a mighty ELOHIYM we serve! If I had not obeyed our Heavenly Father YAHUAH's instruction, there would not have been protection for my family.

In another incident of divine protection, my wife and I were in our car, waiting for another car to move. In the car ahead, a couple was having a domestic dispute. The woman started speeding toward us until her car was directly in front of ours. She was at the point of no return when we felt something move our car away from hers. She was so close to us that we thought we had been hit, and we were amazed when we realized we had not been hit after all. We know angels protected us. Angels hearken to the Word of YAHUAH. Our Heavenly Father YAHUAH is so awesome; we marvel because of who He is.

I truly believe in covering my family with prayer and confessing the Word over my family daily. Our Heavenly Father YAHUAH proved to me the prayers of the righteous avail much, and obedience pays off.

Because you have made YAHUAH, who is my refuge, Even the Most High, your dwelling place,

No evil shall befall you,

Nor shall any plague come near your dwelling;

For He shall give His angels charge over you.

Psalm 91:9-11 NKJV

Our Heavenly Father YAHUAH continued to direct our every step. We started to become comfortable with the way YAHUAH was directing our path. He was faithful time and time again. He would direct us to go to a service at assembly, and it would be exactly what we needed to hear. Our Heavenly Father YAHUAH made it quite clear that I was on His schedule and not my schedule. This is exactly the way it should be, not my way but His way.

We trusted our Heavenly Father YAHUAH even though we didn't know exactly what we were doing or where we were going. We knew we were being directed. Our Heavenly Father YAHUAH was taking care of us. He gave us scripture.

Trust in YAHUAH with all your heart,

And lean not on your own understanding;

In all your ways acknowledge Him,

And He shall direct your paths.

Proverbs 3:5,6 NKJV

For YAHUAH gives wisdom;

From His mouth come knowledge and understanding;

He stores up sound wisdom for the upright;

He is a shield to those who walk uprightly;

He guards the path of justice,

And preserves the way of His saints.

Proverbs 2:6-8 NKJV

I didn't decide to take this path in my life. Our Heavenly Father YAHUAH directed me into the path for His purpose, and I can tell you I am not disappointed. What a meaningless life I was living before! I am seeing people's lives changed, people being healed because we prayed for them, and people receiving YAHUAH as their ADONAI and YAHUSHA as their SAVIOR. I could not be happier and more satisfied with my life. Our Heavenly Father YAHUAH is so good, and He is marvelous in my sight.

Our Heavenly Father YAHUAH started to teach me more about being a doer of the Word and not just a hearer. Before, I was just being obedient to what He was telling me. Now, He wanted me to understand how to apply the Word with purpose. Our Heavenly Father YAHUAH said,

"Believe, speak, and act like every promise is true. I want you to rule and reign over your circumstances."

Our Heavenly Father YAHUAH was teaching me how to keep satan from dominating. YAHUAH was showing me how to seek Him through the Word of YAHUAH. What a wonderful time I started to have with the Word of YAHUAH. The Word was meaning more to me. I was receiving more and more revelation as I read YAHUAH's Word. Our Heavenly Father YAHUAH was teaching me how to not allow my mind to touch what He was directing me to do, but to be led by The RUACH and let my mind catch up later. our Heavenly Father YAHUAH was teaching me how to put pressure on the natural realm with the Word of YAHUAH and get results! He was teaching me that my footsteps were being ordered by the Word of YAHUAH. My head was going crazy, but my ruach was excited all the time. I would start to read a scripture and I would get excited. This seemed strange to me at first. I was at home by myself, not at our place of worship, and I was getting excited because I was reading the Bible. That was when I knew the Word was alive. I had heard others talk about their experiences with the Bible, but now this was my own experience. My ruach would leap inside and I would start to pray in tongues. No one had said a thing to me. It was just from reading! I thought, "This stuff people have told me about is really true! You can get excited all by yourself with your Bible."

I want to talk about the Word of YAHUAH and how important it is that the Word be first in your life. I direct this especially to the men. Most men I have talked with, even believers, put their jobs before their families. Well, I am here to tell you that if you don't provide guidance for your family by praying for them, spending time in the Word, letting our Heavenly Father YAHUAH direct you in the Word pertaining to your family, having devotional time with your family, and taking them to assembly, you are not providing for them. You might bring home a paycheck, but most wives bring home paychecks now too, so you know there must be more to providing than money.

I had plenty of plans for my family, short- and long-term plans, but they were not the plans our Heavenly Father YAHUAH had for me. I had planned on staying in the military for as long as I could, which would have been a long time, but that was not our Heavenly Father YAHUAH's plan for me. I am telling you, you have to take time and find out whether you are on the track our

Heavenly Father YAHUAH wants you on. Your track might look good. You might be providing well for your family, but is it YAHUAH's plan for you?

This is the scripture our Heavenly Father YAHUAH gave me:

And do not be conformed to this world, but be transformed by the renewing of your mind, that you may prove what is that good and acceptable and perfect will of YAHUAH. Romans 12:2 NKJV

Our Heavenly Father YAHUAH taught me how to take good care of my wife. How precious she is to me. I used to think she should just listen to me. But now I also know how to listen to her. I understand that the wisdom of YAHUAH flows through her. We have developed a relationship I know we couldn't have without our Heavenly Father YAHUAH's guidance.

Now, I do not sacrifice my time with her for work or anything else. I know I have to answer to our Heavenly Father YAHUAH on how I treat her and how much time I spend with her. I cannot neglect her for my own needs or to conduct business.

Our Heavenly Father YAHUAH let me know that my wife was not there just to cook my meals, clean the house, watch the children and take care of my physical needs. She had to mean as much to me as I meant to myself.

I did not realize how much I had taken her for granted and to what extent she had been there for me and the children. I had to give her time when she wanted it, and not just when I had time to give to her.

I had to find out what she wanted to do and not just include her in the things I wanted to do. You have to really look at yourself and see how selfish you have been. I can't even begin to tell you everything I had to change, or how much time it took for me to incorporate the changes into a routine. I wanted to please our Heavenly Father YAHUAH and to truly love my wife the way I was supposed to love her according to the Word of YAHUAH.

So husbands ought to love their own wives as their own bodies; he who loves his wife loves himself. For no one ever hated his own flesh, but nourishes and cherishes it, just as YAHUSHA does the church.
Ephesians 5:28, 29 NKJV

our Heavenly Father YAHUAH began to direct us to think more about renewing our wedding vows. Andrea had already purchased a dress for this occasion, so we started to pray about a place and exactly what our Heavenly Father YAHUAH wanted us to do. He was taking care of all of our needs. Now our hearts' desire was to renew our vows. We were different people now, so it made sense to renew our wedding vows. our Heavenly Father YAHUAH had our complete attention and our love. We wanted whatever our Heavenly Father YAHUAH wanted. We wanted to stay in the perfect will of YAHUAH. We said, "YAHUAH, we are living for You. We want Your best in every area of our lives." We also knew our Heavenly Father YAHUAH wanted us to have His best.

This is the scripture our Heavenly Father YAHUAH gave us concerning our desires:

May He grant you according to your heart's desire,
And fulfill all your purpose.
Psalm 20:4 NKJV

One thing I noticed was the closer we grew to our Heavenly Father YAHUAH, the closer we grew to each other. We began to feel we should look for invitations, and we found them right away. Then we knew we were being led to look for a place to have the vows renewed. Andrea started to look for flowers and think about whom we wanted to invite. Our Heavenly Father YAHUAH helped us complete the invitation list and find the person to officiate our vow renewal service. Things came together rather quickly.

During this time, our Heavenly Father YAHUAH had directed us to go pray with a pastor and his wife. While we were praying with them, our Heavenly Father YAHUAH directed us to give them our wedding rings. That very morning the pastor's wife had taken off her wedding ring because she had lost weight and it no longer fit her finger. She had also believed our Heavenly Father YAHUAH for a two-and-a-half-karat ring, which was exactly the weight of my wife's ring. After our Heavenly Father YAHUAH instructed us to give the rings to them, we were in awe of the pastor's wife's testimony. She had been believing our Heavenly Father YAHUAH for the same weight of ring that my wife had. We knew our Heavenly Father YAHUAH wanted to bless them, and we were as happy as they were.

We felt it was an honor to give away the rings, because our Heavenly Father YAHUAH had blessed us with them anyway. We thought YAHUAH was going to give us a new set of rings before we said our vows, because people just didn't perform weddings without wedding rings. We were sure our ceremony would not be performed without rings either.

Days passed and no rings appeared. We continued to ask our Heavenly Father YAHUAH for a place to have our vows renewed, and He directed us to a country club.

We called to get information and find out what we needed to do. We also checked out other places and waited to see exactly where our Heavenly Father YAHUAH wanted us to be.

One morning we were thanking our Heavenly Father YAHUAH for a place to have our vows and I said, "YAHUAH we need an answer today." I opened the telephone book to look for more possible places, and the lady from the country club called us.

When she and I had talked previously, she had told me it would take a thousand dollars to hold the hall, and she was calling now to let me know we did not have to put the thousand dollars down after all. So we went to the country club, made the plans, and selected the date to renew our vows. We were so excited! This was such a beautiful place.

Andrea went to the flower shop to decide what kind of flowers she wanted to have for the ceremony. While she was there, she also saw some flowers she would like to have for our house. Her thought was simply that she would love to have those flowers at home. She never said anything aloud, she only thought about it.

By the time Andrea returned home, the flowers were in her room. The manager of our building had heard about the renewing of our vows, and they had ordered the flowers for her. Remember now, she never told anyone! our Heavenly Father YAHUAH just put it on the hearts of the people to buy the flowers and send them to her. Andrea was awestruck. She just kept looking at the flowers and saying, "How did these get here?"

I told her, "The building manager ordered them." She said, "You don't understand. I just thought about having the same flowers at home just a few minutes before I got home." The flowers had made it home before she did. Our Heavenly Father YAHUAH is an awesome ELOHIYM.

Our Heavenly Father YAHUAH was continuing to give us the desires of our hearts.

We finished mailing the invitations to all the people on the list, which YAHUAH had placed on our hearts. We ended up with about eighty people attending our marriage vow renewal celebration. We had a wonderful time. My wife was beautiful. She took my breath away. I was speechless when I saw her.

During the time we were supposed to exchange our rings (we hadn't yet been blessed with rings to replace the rings we had given away), we honored our Heavenly Father YAHUAH for our marriage and for what He had done in our lives. We made sure everyone knew YAHUSHA was the center of everything good in our lives.

We gave YAHUSHA all the credit for our successful marriage and our wonderful family. YAHUSHA got the glory! It didn't seem to matter about the rings. We knew our Heavenly Father YAHUAH had a higher purpose that night.

I surprised Andrea with a horse and buggy ride, something she had always wanted. The associate pastor of our place of worship officiated in the ceremony. A lady from our place of worship sang, we took communion, and we lit a unity candle. Even the unity candle has its special story. We had looked for a particular unity candle, and our Heavenly Father YAHUAH directed Andrea to a particular store. She did not see what she was looking for, but when she asked the clerk, she went into the back room and came out with exactly what Andrea wanted. We feel YAHUAH hides and saves things just for us. Our Heavenly Father YAHUAH certainly put everything together for our marriage vow renewal celebration. We had such a blessed time. We couldn't imagine how or even whether this event would have taken place if we were not in YAHUAH's life. Our Heavenly Father YAHUAH helped us in every area, from the music to the best food. It was like being in a storybook or a dream. I really felt as though I was dreaming. I just thought our Heavenly Father YAHUAH was so good to us, and we wanted so much to please Him!

Let them shout for joy and be glad,
Who favor my righteous cause;
And let them say continually,
"Let YAHUAH be magnified,
Who has pleasure in the prosperity of His servant. "
Psalm 35:27 NKJV

We had made financial arrangements with someone for a portion of the provision for our wedding renewal ceremony. However, things did not turn out exactly as we thought they should.

We were confused about the outcome of the situation, so we did what we always do in every situation. We took it to YAHUAH in prayer because we understand YAHUAH is not an ELOHIYM of confusion.

Meanwhile, our friend had gone to our place of worship and brought us back a tape of a sermon on dream stealers. Glory to YAHUAH! What a sermon. We were so blessed. It brought such understanding of what was going on in our situation. Our Heavenly Father YAHUAH will give you understanding of a situation and you will have peace. There are times in your life that satan will attack you because you have exalted YAHUSHA. But we know we have the victory. We had exalted YAHUSHA all night long when we renewed our vows. The enemy didn't like that, but our Heavenly Father YAHUAH gave us a scripture, as always, to help us stand strong.

And we know that all things work together for good to those who love YAHUAH, to those who are the called according to His purpose.

Romans 8:28 NKJV

And the ELOHYIM of peace will crush satan under your feet shortly.
The grace of our ADONAI YAHUSHA HA'MASHIACH be with you. Amen.
Romans 16:20 NKJV

You might think we needed money because the financial arrangement didn't turn out of the way we had planned. However, we needed only to understand how to handle the enemy, satan, with the Word of YAHUAH.

If we didn't know how to deal with attacks, satan, would defeat us all the time. We needed to mature in the Word of YAHUAH. We spent more time in the Word of YAHUAH, more time in prayer, and more time learning how to reinforce satan's defeat.

We went to assembly on a Saturday night, and the minister said anyone who had financial problems should come up for prayer. We didn't move an inch because we didn't feel we needed prayer. Our circumstances were saying we had financial problems, but we felt as though everything was taken care of. We wondered what we were experiencing, because neither one of us went forward for prayer. The pastor explained when your circumstances say one thing negative and you are feeling totally different, or positive, about your situation, it is called "inward sufficiency." He said that means you believe what YAHUAH has said, and not your circumstances. We were so happy because we knew our Heavenly Father YAHUAH had led us to this assembly again that night to hear a Word from Him. Our Heavenly Father YAHUAH always had protected us. We felt so much love and protection from our Heavenly Father YAHUAH.

And YAHUAH is able to make all grace abound toward you, that you always have all sufficiency in all things, may have an abundance for every good work.
2 Corinthians 9:8 NKJV

We were really happy now with our progress in the Word of YAHUAH. We now had inward sufficiency. Our circumstances were not controlling us, and we believed the Word of YAHUAH, not our feelings.

We understood if we would take the Word of YAHUAH and apply it to our situation, that would give YAHUAH free reign to turn our situation around for us. If we did not do this, then we would give satan free reign to bring the negative to pass in our lives.

There is no faith without the Word of YAHUAH. A scripture exists for every situation you experience.

For the word of YAHUAH is living and powerful, and sharper than any two-edged sword, piercing even to the division of soul and ruach, and of joints and marrow, and is a discerner of the thoughts and intents of the heart. Hebrews 4:12 NKJV

We learned the Word searches us and wherever we need to be changed, the Word will change us. It will also change our outward circumstances, and they will line up with the word of YAHUAH. That is what the "two-edged sword" meant to us. It changes us inside, and it changes outward circumstances in the natural realm. We experienced this time and time again.

We continued to grow in our Heavenly Father and to experience His grace and mercy in our lives. YAHUAH took care of the financial obligation concerning our wedding renewal, and we learned a lot in the process. After about six months, our Heavenly Father YAHUAH started to impress upon us, that He wanted us to attend a convention out of town.

During this time, Andrea had a list of things we needed in order for us to take the trip. We needed airfare and someone to watch the children. The person had to love our Heavenly Father YAHUAH, already know the children, and have a driver's license. Our Heavenly Father YAHUAH took care of the airfare. Andrea went to our place of worship to attend a meeting, and a young woman we knew came up to her and said, "I had quit my job. I just got my driver's license. I am supposed to be a nanny for your boys."

I tell you; I am not kidding. Andrea called me, and I could hardly understand what she was talking about because she was so in awe of our Heavenly Father YAHUAH. The young lady was one of our sons' bible school teachers.

Our sons adored her, and we were also very fond of her. YAHUAH answered my wife's request in such a specific way that we were just amazed. We loved our Heavenly Father YAHUAH so much and He was continuing to show His love for us.

As we continued to trust and obey our Heavenly Father YAHUAH, He continued to put us to the test of trusting Him with our whole hearts (our ruachs), souls (our minds, wills and emotions), and bodies. He wanted all, not some of our trust.

Our Heavenly Father YAHUAH provided everything we needed for the trip. This was a very different trip. We had a credit card but only twenty dollars of pocket money.

Chapter Eight

~ ~ ~ ~ ~ ~ ~ ~ ~

Fullness Of Joy – Andrea

I was so apprehensive about going on this trip because I had never gone out of town with only twenty dollars before. And this time, I really didn't want to leave the kids. My ruach was willing, but my carnal nature was having a heyday. I just said, "YAHUAH, help me".

Even though two of my friends had said they would check in on the boys, I was still having a hard time. But when we got on the airplane, our Heavenly Father YAHUAH said to me, "To much is given, much is required." All of a sudden, I had total peace with my ruach and my mind. Our Heavenly Father YAHUAH had spoken to me, and that was all I needed. Sometimes you need time to rest. We needed this time away more than I had realized.

As soon as we arrived at our destination airport, Melvin went to the counter to rent a car and the credit card did not work. He went to another counter and the credit card still did not work, so Melvin left that counter and came to talk with me. We stopped and prayed to see what was going on and what our Heavenly Father YAHUAH was doing now. My cousin had just moved to this town, and our Heavenly Father YAHUAH told me to call her. I didn't have her telephone number, but I had given the number to Melvin before we left home and he had decided to bring the number along. I called my cousin and told her our credit card did not work.

She told us that YAHUAH does not like ugly and the credit card had done exactly as it should have done. She came to get us, and we stayed at her house. We didn't want to bother her because we knew she had just moved there and was probably still getting settled but we had planned to call her toward the end of our trip.

As you have probably guessed by now, our Heavenly Father YAHUAH had better plans. We loved my cousin's new house. It was beautiful.

I am really fond of my cousin and her family, and we had a great time with them. Melvin had mentioned to me on the plane that he wanted a good hot meal, and I had said I would like a refrigerator full of food. Well, when we got to my cousin's house, she decided she needed to prepare a good hot meal. I looked in her refrigerator and our

Heavenly Father YAHUAH said, "Here is your refrigerator full of food."

YAHUAH can answer your needs in so many ways that your mind cannot understand. When we got up the next morning, my cousin told us how to get to the conference. We were to take the train that went to the airport, then a bus to the conference. From the moment we got on the train, our Heavenly Father YAHUAH spoke to my ruach and said, "This is what you have always said you wanted, to take a train across town."

Again, our Heavenly Father YAHUAH was giving me a desire of my heart. If the credit card had worked, we would have gotten a rental car and a hotel room. I would not have had the opportunity to spend time with my cousin, and I certainly would not have been taking a train. This was so wonderful.

You know, YAHUAH likes to surprise us, but sometimes He cannot surprise us because we want to know all the details before we budge. As you can tell by my experiences, you will miss a lot of what our Heavenly Father YAHUAH has for you if you don't cooperate and flow with The RUACH HA'QODESH.

During the first couple of days of the conference, we met a pastor who was sitting behind Melvin. The two men began to talk. The pastor told Melvin to come follow him and he told me to also come. He told us he needed to take us to lunch.

We had only twenty dollars, so we gladly accepted his invitation. We went to the pastor's car and started to ride down the street. The next thing we knew, he began to prophesy to us. We knew what he was saying was true because he knew nothing about us, and it was complete confirmation to us. This pastor was driving a debt-free Jaguar. He said this was where our Heavenly Father YAHUAH was taking us in our life, to debt-free living because we had sacrificed so much to follow our Heavenly Father YAHUAH. He started to command all these blessings on our life.

The anointing in that car was so thick that we felt as though we were in an assembly full of people. The anointing fell on Melvin and me, and we started to repeat the blessing over our lives. We received all our Heavenly Father YAHUAH was giving us.

After the pastor finished telling us everything he had to say, he said our Heavenly Father YAHUAH had never used him in that way before. When we finished lunch, he asked us if we would go to his assembly with him to pray. We said yes, and when we were there, he asked us if we would pray over him, which we did. We also anointed him with oil, and he told us this was not something he usually did either. We said we knew our Heavenly Father YAHUAH wanted us to do this because He was always using us to minister to pastors. We returned to the conference and we had a wonderful time in YAHUAH. We left a little early because the pastor had a toothache. He said he had to go to the dentist the next day. We asked him if we could pray for him, and he said yes. We prayed, and when he started to bite down on his teeth, the pain was gone! Glory to YAHUAH! What an awesome ELOHIYM we serve.

Let me tell you a little more about our visit at my cousin's house. She had a bed I used whenever I visited her. It is my favorite bed, so you know our Heavenly Father YAHUAH wanted me to sleep in it, and of course I did. Also, each morning Melvin and I had whatever we wanted to eat. More importantly, we got to spend time with my cousin and her family, whom we love. I would get up in the morning and said, "Thank you, YAHUAH, I always wanted to spend more time with my cousin." We would come home every night to a delicious dinner she made or had taken the time to order for us. The provision was tremendous. our Heavenly Father YAHUAH supplied our needs, and he gave us the desires of our hearts.

If you are willing and obedient, you shall eat the good of the land.
Isaiah 1:19 NKJV

The next day at the conference, the anointing was tremendous, and something happened to me that had never happened before. I went up to the front of the assembly and I sat on my knees. I started to make wonderful movements with my hands. I opened my eyes and there were only women up there doing the same thing. What a beautiful time it was. It was as though we were moving and making music with our hands just for our Heavenly Father YAHUAH.

It was now time for lunch, and we were waiting to find out what our Heavenly Father YAHUAH wanted us to do. Many people asked us if we needed a ride or if they could give us a ride. We didn't feel that our Heavenly Father YAHUAH wanted us to leave the assembly, so we kept turning down rides. The assembly seemed to be totally empty except for the security guard. He asked us if we were waiting for someone, and we didn't know what to say. Usually, they would not let people stay in the assembly until the next meeting. Yet, the security guard said we could stay, and he would tell the guards it was okay that we were still there.

By the time the next session began, the pastors who were teaching at the time stood up in front of the whole assembly congregation and told us they were going to prophesy over us. We were to repeat for ourselves what they were saying. our Heavenly Father YAHUAH told us He had us stay in the assembly so we could fast, so we could receive the impartation. We were happy that we had followed the leading we were receiving from The RUACH HA'QODESH and had not left the assembly to go to lunch.

All we have to do is follow that leading or listen to the still small voice, that witness we have in our inner man. Four pastors were in front of all us. They spoke words of healing, prosperity, and holiness to all of us. "YAHUAH is my shepherd, I shall not want," Psalm 23:1, came up in my ruach. I thought, "I haven't heard this scripture in a long time."

It was like scrolls in front of me in the RUACH. I saw everything our Heavenly Father YAHUAH had told Melvin and me we were going to have so far in our lives. It was so amazing. I told a lady at the conference what I saw, and she said, "Well, you have been sowing and that is your harvest." I didn't know this lady; she was just sitting next to me. It had to be revelation knowledge. I was so excited that I didn't know what to do.

I had heard people say the Word of YAHUAH was pregnant, that it continues to grow. I began shouting it was harvest time, because we certainly had heard all week that you can have what you say if you only believe and do not doubt.

For let not that man suppose that he will receive anything from YAHUAH; he is a double-minded man, unstable in all his ways.
James 1:7,8 NKJV

We confessed all kinds of things over our families and our business. We had a wonderful time in our Heavenly Father YAHUAH. It was such an uplifting time and refreshing to listen to the Word of YAHUAH with such compassion and zeal from men of YAHUAH.

It was time for us to go back to my cousin's house, and she had told us she would pick us up. But there was a couple there whom I couldn't take my eyes off. We were leaving from the same area of the assembly and I started talking with the lady. She offered to take us to the train, so I decided I wouldn't bother my cousin. When we were in the car with the lady and her husband, the anointing came on me so strong that I asked the man to pull over so I could pray for them. The couple had been asking our Heavenly Father YAHUAH for prosperity and healing and when I prayed, all of what they had been asking for came out in prayer. It was total confirmation for them, so they drove us all the way home. They were so thankful that we had obeyed the prompting of The RUACH HA'QODESH. And by this time, we realized that if we had rented a car, none of these things would have happened. We would not have been in the cars with all these wonderful people of YAHUAH. What had seemed like an inconvenience at first turned out to be blessing for everyone. Most of all, we saw how purposeful our Heavenly Father YAHUAH is and how much He cares for each and every one of His children.

What a loving and concerned Father our Heavenly Father YAHUAH is. All He wants are willing vessels to help Him carry out His plans. Melvin and I were certainly happy that we were two of the people our Heavenly Father YAHUAH let in on how awesome, loving and good He is! What a wonderful plan He has for His children's lives.

The next day at the conference, we saw the pastor and his wife whom we had ministered to the year before. We enjoyed talking with them and catching up on things. Our Heavenly Father YAHUAH had them sow a seed into us. What a wonderful and precious ELOHIYM we serve.

We were happy that they were still in the ministry, and they started their own assembly that YAHUAH had instructed them to start. The devil hadn't been able to steal what seed had been sown into them the previous year.

We needed a ride home again, so we talked with some people at the assembly, and they said they would find someone to take us home. They told us to wait in the front of the assembly. We did this, and all of a sudden, a young man came out and said he wanted to give us a ride home. We told him he could take us to the train, we didn't mind, we liked taking the train. But he insisted on taking us back to my cousin's house. The next thing we knew, we were outside. There was a Lincoln Town Car and the young man was urging us to get in the back seat of the car.

We said, "That's okay, Melvin will ride up front with you."

The young man told us he wanted to serve us, that he was the driver from the pastor of the assembly we were visiting. I thought, "YAHUAH, what are you doing?" I couldn't believe what was happening. The pastor of this assembly at the conference was a very well-known pastor. We said, "YAHUAH, you have outdone yourself now." You cannot beat our Heavenly Father YAHUAH's giving. What a giver YAHUAH is! All we did was obey, and the blessings of YAHUAH were chasing us down and overtaking us. We were so awestruck that we could barely speak when we got back to my cousin's house. We kept looking at each other, wondering what had just happened.

When our Heavenly Father YAHUAH blesses you, sometimes you wonder, "How can I ever pay you back, YAHUAH?" You feel as though you just want to do something so wonderful for our Heavenly Father YAHUAH. But you know you can't do anything that can even touch the way He blesses. We could not have planned a better trip.

On our most creative day, we could not have come up with anything this fulfilling, satisfying or full of as much love as

YAHUAH showed for his children that week. To YAHUAH be the glory forever and ever. Amen.

After our wonderful time in our Heavenly Father YAHUAH, satan tried to show up. I say "tried" because by now, our Heavenly Father YAHUAH had shown us too much to even fall for satan and his tactics. We knew our Heavenly Father YAHUAH would bless us. But then satan would attack and try to move us off of the Word our Heavenly Father YAHUAH had given us. We knew we wanted to serve YAHUAH with all of our hearts, our souls and our minds. We knew our Heavenly Father YAHUAH was a merciful and just ELOHIYM. We knew He had the hearts of His children in mind. We were going to do everything we could to serve our Heavenly Father YAHUAH.

Therefore humble yourselves under the mighty hand of YAHUAH, that he may exalt you in due time, casting all your care upon Him, for He cares for you.

Be sober, be vigilant; because your adversary the devil walks about like a roaring lion, seeking whom he may devour. Resist him, steadfast in the faith, knowing that the same sufferings are experienced by your brotherhood in the world. But may the ELOHIYM of all grace, who called us to His eternal glory by MASHIACH YAHUSHA, after you have suffered a while, perfect establish, strengthen and settle you.

1 Peter 5:6-10 NKJV

I think sometimes we forget we are not the only ones paying a price to follow after YAHUSHA HA'MASHIACH. We tend to think of our own circumstances as really bad, and certainly no one else can be as bad off as we are. YAHUAH Almighty is more powerful than satan. The devil has no power over the righteous. He was stripped of his power over two thousand years ago.

I thank our Heavenly Father YAHUAH for reminding me satan can bring only contrary circumstances into my life and it is up to me to believe either the Word of YAHUAH or my circumstance.

The Word of YAHUAH is like a medicine to me, and it is up to me whether I want to be set free or not. We are always checking ourselves to make sure we are not doing anything to give satan permission to come into our lives.

The devil will attack you when you are in the complete will of YAHUAH, to try to get you off track and make you think YAHUAH doesn't care about you. If he can convince you YAHUAH doesn't care about you, satan will win you over, but he cannot control you if your decision is to follow YAHUAH.

Our Heavenly Father YAHUAH had used us many times to bless other people with finances and other things they needed in their lives, and they would be blessed.

Give, and it will be given to you: good measures, pressed down, shaken together, and running over will be put into your bosom. For with the same measure that you use, it will be measured back to you.
Luke 6:38 NKJV

Our Heavenly Father YAHUAH would have us buy things for other people and we would not even know who it was for. We would have something at our houses and our Heavenly Father YAHUAH would tell us to give it to a certain person, and it would be exactly what they had been believing YAHUAH for. We would buy things for others, such as housewarming gifts or a birthday gifts, and it would be just what they needed. Or it would complete the set for something they already had at their house.

Chapter Nine

~ ~ ~ ~ ~ ~ ~ ~ ~ ~

Be Bold, Be Strong!

We also had, and still have victory for healing in our family. As an example, I had a bump under my arm, and I couldn't get rid of it. Part of the bump would leave, but another part would stay. I finally asked our Heavenly Father YAHUAH, "How can I get rid of this so it will not come back?"

I was in a service at a assembly we were visiting when a lady said to me, "Do you know that bump under your arm? You need to put a slice of potato under your arm and that will get rid of it." This sounded very strange to me, but this lady and I did not even know each other. So, I went home and put the potato under my arm, and I immediately felt the potato pulling the impurities out. After doing this every night for a week, the bump was gone, and it never returned.

Not long after that I felt a sharp pain in my stomach, and I knew satan was just trying to get me to agree with what he was trying to put on me. The pain was so intense that I was doubled over, and I said only what the Word of YAHUAH says, by YAHUSHA's stripes I am healed the attacks of the enemy cannot overcome me. I then started to pray in The RUACH, and the pain left immediately. Glory be to YAHUAH, our Heavenly Father our ELOHIYM! The devil could not and cannot stand against the Word of YAHUAH. Now that the Word was working in our lives and we had victory in every area of our lives, satan was in trouble. Now we understood what to do with his attacks.

Do the Word and listen to the directions of The RUACH HA'QODESH. Our Heavenly Father YAHUAH had taught us how to use the Word of YAHUAH in every situation and to listen for the direction of The RUACH HA'QODESH.

After the attacks from satan, our Heavenly Father YAHUAH had a woman at our place of worship give us an envelope containing one thousand three hundred sixty dollars in cash. She told us our Heavenly Father YAHUAH wanted her to give it to us. We told her we had been attacked in our finances and she said, "Praise our Heavenly Father YAHUAH!" She knew we were the right people to receive the money. Every time the enemy attacked us, our Heavenly Father YAHUAH did a counterattack much greater than anything satan could do. Our Heavenly Father YAHUAH is so worthy to be praised! He promises us, wherever He sends us, He will provide, and He always has.

I do not know what happened for that woman after she gave us that money, but every time she would see us after that, she would say, "You are a blessing." She was a very happy woman. We had never seen her smile so much. YAHUAH must have been very good to her because of her obedience to what He had told her to do. Our Heavenly Father YAHUAH always rewards obedience to what He tells you to do.

Our Heavenly Father YAHUAH kept reminding us that He is the provider. He directed us to visit a couple we knew. The husband wasn't home, and the woman had to leave with her infant to pick up her other children from an event they were attending. She also had other errands to run, but she was having car trouble. Our Heavenly Father YAHUAH wanted us to take her so we did, but we needed gas money.

Earlier that day the woman had said that if someone would take her to run her errands, she would give them gas. What a good match! She needed a car and we needed gas. We prayed for her and her family. The next day at our place of worship, her husband came up to my husband and gave him a check for a thousand dollars. The man said, "Thank you for taking care of my wife."

Do you think our Heavenly Father YAHUAH was telling satan, "The more you attack my children, the more I will take care of them, the more I will bless them"? We knew we were in right standing with our Heavenly Father YAHUAH and doing everything He asked us to the best of our ability. He always added His ability to it.

One day Melvin was telling our Heavenly Father YAHUAH he wanted to take his family out to lunch. That same day, a lady learned over to us at our place of worship and said, "This is for you." It was a check for six hundred dollars. Do you think that was enough for Melvin to take his family out to lunch? The lady had just felt like blessing him.

Our Heavenly Father YAHUAH said He would pour you out a blessing that you could barely contain. We were overwhelmed by the goodness of YAHUAH. We knew satan did not have any place in our lives, and our Heavenly Father YAHUAH was certainly rebuking the devourer for our sake. YAHUAH is an awesome ELOHIYM!

Melvin wanted to go to an Aviation Expo because he is a pilot. I used to say, "We don't have the money," but I can't even use those words anymore. All I can say is "The money is not in our hands at the moment." Well, Melvin told his Father in Heaven that he wanted to go to the Expo, and this is how it came about: We went over to a small airport to pray. Suddenly a man came up and knocked on our car window and Melvin got out to talk with him. The man had been having car trouble, and the two men together could not get his car started. The man told Melvin he would give him a ride to the Expo, and he would pay our way in. It is just like our Heavenly Father YAHUAH to match people up with other people who have needs. We needed tickets and he needed a car. We learned the man had fallen away from our Heavenly Father YAHUAH. We talked to him, and he said he was going to consider coming back to our Heavenly Father YAHUAH. YAHUAH has purpose in everything He does. Our lives are so rich now, and full of life in YAHUAH. We could not have imagined the wonderful lives our Heavenly Father YAHUAH had in store for us.

And who is he who will harm you if you become followers of what is good? But even if you should suffer for

righteousness' sake you are blessed. And do not be afraid
of their threats, nor be troubled. But sanctify YAHUAH the
MASHIACH in your hearts, and always be ready to give a
defense to everyone who asks you a reason for the hope
that is in you.
1 Peter 3:13-15 NKJV

Please remember, most of our suffering was in our minds
because we were learning to do things YAHUAH's way
and not the way we had learned in the past. It is sometimes
difficult to change the way you have been thinking for a
long time.

It was a change to believe YAHUAH instead of the
wisdom of people who didn't understand YAHUAH's way
of doing things. Sometimes people we greatly respected
had given us advice in the past. But when their advice goes
against what our Heavenly Father YAHUAH is telling you
and you are certain it is YAHUAH speaking, you have to
go with YAHUAH. You can't feel guilty about it or feel as
though you are disrespecting the people giving you advice.
You just have to obey YAHUAH. I learned a long time
ago that it is not about a felling. It is about YAHUAH.

We had to speak the Word when we wanted to talk about circumstances. We had to keep our mouths closed when we wanted to say something to someone who had treated us wrongly. We had to wait and do everything YAHUAH's way and not our way. Our Heavenly Father YAHUAH had perfect timing, and it was not easy to wait on our Heavenly Father YAHUAH's timing. But we had seen too many people who had not waited, and it was not pretty. We had truly learned how to be patient. When you wait on our Heavenly Father YAHUAH, you will develop patience which will help you the next time.

Our Heavenly Father YAHUAH had us move in with a friend. She told us that when we moved in, a lot of pressure was relieved from her. We learned so much about faith because we continued to flow with our Heavenly Father YAHUAH without complete understanding. During this time, all we did was obey The RUACH HA'QODESH. Our Heavenly Father YAHUAH touched us in a way He had not touched us before. The love, warmth, peace, joy, and wisdom of YAHUAH started flowing like a river through our ruachs, united with The RUACH of the living ELOHIYM. We were in awe of the essence of YAHUAH. We were becoming beings of YAHUAH, one with Him and His purpose for our lives. He had truly united us with Him.

We had The RUACH of MASHIACH from our experience with YAHUAH and His perfect will for our lives. We were living lives totally yielded to our Heavenly Father YAHUAH. It started to get easier because we were yielded and more understanding to His ways and His direction. We had compassion for people in a different way because we had the mind of MASHIACH. What a wonderful and truly pleasant feeling to be in one accord with YAHUAH the Father, YAHUSHA HA'MASHIACH, and The RUACH HA'QODESH. The Word of YAHUAH was so deep in our ruachs that now it would automatically come out of our mouths.

During this time the scripture "YAHUAH is my Shepherd, I shall not want" came to us again. our Heavenly Father YAHUAH instructed us to take communion and receive everything back that we had left to follow Him. We were instructed to receive everything back a hundredfold and receive it under the blood of YAHUSHA. And we did. Praise the name of the ADONIA YAHUSHA HA'MASHIACH. Amen.

We knew there was no lack in our lives because we had YAHUAH, YAHUSHA HA'MASHIACH, and The RUACH HA'QODESH with us. We knew all of heaven was backing us in all we were doing.

This is the scripture our Heavenly Father YAHUAH gave us:

If you can believe, all things are possible to him who believes.
Mark 9:23 NKJV

It was time to move on with the direction of The RUACH HA'QODESH. My mother wanted us to come stay with her, so we moved into my mother's house. After we moved, our Heavenly Father YAHUAH directed a friend and me to attend a convention in New York. One of our friends worked for an airline, and I ended up paying only sixty dollars round trip.

During this time our Heavenly Father YAHUAH had me ministering to pastors again. They always knew I had a Word from our Heavenly Father YAHUAH. He would tell me whom to talk to, and the Word I spoke would always be just what the pastors needed from our Heavenly Father YAHUAH. What I spoke confirmed their prayers and answered their questions, they said. This proves all you need to do is be a willing vessel for our Heavenly Father YAHUAH.

During the offering at the convention, our Heavenly Father YAHUAH had me give money to the entire row of people I was sitting in for their offerings, and also to others behind me. And that led to other things. He had me give the young woman next to me my scarf and my earrings; they were my favorites. Next, my friend gave her ring to someone next to her and the young woman gave me her earrings. There was a mighty move of The RUACH HA'QODESH going on, and the ministers had not even started to preach yet. Everyone who had given something to someone else said it was their favorite thing they had just given away. When the minister started to preach the message, he asked, "Can you give up something that you really like?" Our Heavenly Father YAHUAH had confirmed the message before it even started. We had a good time giving.

Do not be deceived, YAHUAH is not mocked; for whatever a man sows, that he will also reap
Galatians 6:7 NKJV

While the earth remains,

Seedtime and harvest,

Cold and heat,

Winter and summer,

And day and night

Shall not cease.

Genesis 8:22 NKJV

Cast your bread upon the waters,

For you will find it after many days.

Ecclesiastes 11:1 NKJV

Now may He who supplies seed to the sower, and bread for food, supply and multiply the seed you have sown and increase the fruits of your righteousness.

2 Corinthians 9:10 NKJV

Our Heavenly Father YAHUAH will give you everything you need, desire, and want if you are lined up with His purpose and His will, because your desires will be His desires. I always wanted to do a special for our television show. Our Heavenly Father YAHUAH gave me a vision of what the show should look like and the people He wanted in the show. He also gave me the atmosphere of the show. I saw angels going into the stores we taped in. The angels went before us to prepare the way. I said, YAHUAH, if you want me to do this, I desire the provision."

A businessman whom we had talked with in the summer about sponsorship called us from Europe. He was there on business. He said he just had to call and let us know he would give us the sponsorship when he returned home. We talked with all of the people we wanted on the show, and they all agreed to be on the show. We had everyone we needed for production. As you know, if our Heavenly Father YAHUAH is your director, the show will be a success, and it was. Our Heavenly Father YAHUAH said, "Your success is in Me."

YAHUAH's hand was on everything. When we purchased our airtime, we received a discount. The manager blocked our airtime before we gave him any money. We needed a piano player. There just happened to be one at one of the malls where we were taping, and she agreed to play for us. A Salvation Army bell ringer helped us unload our equipment. We did not ask him; he approached us. He said, "I am supposed to help you unload this." YAHUAH will provide where He sends you. YAHUAH had many plans for us. We only had to be in His perfecting timing. Most of the timing is used to develop us in Him, to gain His nature and His ways. He wanted us directed, not driven.

YAHUAH was with Joseph, and he was a successful man; and he was in the house of his master the Egyptian. And his master saw that YAHUAH was with him and that YAHUAH made all he did to prosper in his hand.
Genesis 39:2,3 NKJV

Our Heavenly Father YAHUAH always had purpose in what He was doing with us and with the people He chose to be on our shows. He had us pray with some people and minister His Word to others. He used many of our shows when it was time for people and their gifts to come forth. The point is that because we followed Him and His direction, every show was a success and people's lives were changed. This was just behind the scenes. I am sure people's lives were changed through the shows when they were on television because people told us their lives had been touched.

And you shall remember YAHUAH your ELOHIYM, for it is He who gives you power to get wealth, that He may establish His covenant which He swore to your fathers, as it is this day.

Deuteronomy 8:18 NKJV

Success, money, peace, happiness, and love always follow the wisdom of YAHUAH. The success we should feel is from pleasing YAHUAH and knowing YAHUAH is pleased with us. True success is doing the will of the Father.

A faithful man will abound with blessings, but he who hastens to be rich will not go unpunished.
Proverbs 28:20 NKJV

A woman, after being one of our guests on one of our television shows, said our show reminded her of how it used to be when our Heavenly Father YAHUAH was in charge of our assembly services. People were excited. In expectancy with oneness of heart, nothing was more important than to please our Heavenly Father YAHUAH. She also said she saw us trusting and relying on YAHUAH to provide what we needed, rather than relying on ourselves to produce anything.

Her comments continued. She said we created an atmosphere of acceptance and compassion our guests felt when they entered the room. She explained that we were under submission and reliance to The RUACH

HA'QODESH, constantly aware that YAHUAH was in charge. She said "I saw favor on the show to the point of supplying everything from money, to food, to supplies we needed for people. Andrea was in the complete flow of The RUACH HA'QODESH." Her daughter said, "Andrea was glowing. It was a YAHUAH-inspired setup. There was no confusion."

What a tribute to the Father and to The RUACH HA'QODESH. There is nothing like being directed by The RUACH HA'QODESH and carrying The RUACH of YAHUSHA HA'MASHIACH with you. Another woman on location said she had never seen so many things being supplied. She had used this facility and had been in this area for seven years, and she had never before seen this kind of provision. She was in awe of YAHUAH and His provision. She said I had been telling her about the provision of YAHUAH, but this time she saw it for herself. Our Heavenly Father YAHUAH had purpose in the places where we taped our shows and in the people who would be on our shows.

Our Heavenly Father YAHUAH is good and His mercy endures forever. I just had to say that, because I am so happy about our Heavenly Father YAHUAH, His goodness, and how faithful He is to His promises and His purpose. All we have to do is follow His direction and be faithful to what He is telling us to do.

You know how sometimes there is just joy and love bubbling inside of you and you just have to let it out. It is your ruach needing to be released. Just release that laughter, or cry, whatever you need to do. Just do it.

My ruach is soaring, writing this book and thinking on every good thing our Heavenly Father YAHUAH has done for us. I just can't praise Him or thank Him enough for being there for us unconditionally. His promises are true, and He has never broken a promise to us. He has always come through.

When we confessed His Word, as long as we didn't give up, our Heavenly Father YAHUAH didn't give up. Our Heavenly Father YAHUAH never gives up. Only people let go to YAHUAH's promises. But don't let go! Sometimes I would say, "This pressure is just too much for me." Then our Heavenly Father YAHUAH would flood me with His love and His anointing. In His presence, I would have peace and joy. There is no high in comparison to the feeling of being in the presence of our Heavenly

Father YAHUAH. Being high on YAHUSHA is the best for me.

If you have not experienced our Heavenly Father YAHUAH in this way, just ask Him for this kind of intimacy. He is not a respecter of persons. If He did it for me, He will do it for you. I am just tearing up, thinking about how good, loving, and faithful our Heavenly Father YAHUAH has been to me, my husband and my entire family.

We could not imagine a life without YAHUAH, YAHUSHA and The RUACH HA'QODESH. YAHUSHA is such a good example for us of compassion and courage, endurance and love. The RUACH HA'QODESH is the best director and teacher we have ever had. YAHUSHA said in Matthew 22:37, "You shall love YAHUAH your ELOHIYM with all your heart, with all your soul, and with all your mind."

Chapter Ten

~ ~ ~ ~ ~ ~ ~ ~ ~ ~

Speaking The Word – Melvin

Our Heavenly Father YAHUAH directed us to go to a place of worship we had visited before. A speaker there talked about confessions and how important they were to our lives. This helped me to develop the habit of confessing the Word of YAHUAH over my family every morning. I had always prayed. Our Heavenly Father YAHUAH had already directed me to use the Word in every area of my life, so this was not hard to do.

I now have one hundred seventy scriptures I confess over my family every morning. I am always adding more as we get revelation to the Word of YAHUAH. I am now framing our lives with the Word of YAHUAH and creating the lives our Heavenly Father YAHUAH wants us to have.

A few months later, The RUACH YAHUAH spoke to me about my confession, saying I was no longer just confessing the Word, but now I was dominating with the Word of YAHUAH. The Word was now controlling the circumstances of our lives in the natural realm, but the

HEAVENLY REALM is more real than the natural realm. In fact, the HEAVENLY REALM brings impact and change in this natural realm we live in. Needless to say, I was extremely excited about what I was doing, and it strengthened my desire to seek YAHUAH.

The scriptures are working in every area of our lives, and we are seeing the manifestation of the scriptures all the time.

May He grant you out of the rich treasury of His glory to be strengthened and reinforced with mighty power in the inner man.
Ephesians 3:16 AMPC

For the Word that YAHUAH speaks is alive and full of power [making it active, operative, energizing, and effective].
Hebrews 4:12 AMPC

When I confess the Word of YAHUAH over my family and pray, my wife sits next to me and sometimes she gets the complete interpretation of what I am praying in tongues.

For if I pray in a tongue, my ruach prays, but my understanding is unfruitful.

1 Corinthians 14:14 NKJV

We have an awesome time praying together. Now I want to take the time to talk with the men a little more.

I have dedicated my life to our Heavenly Father YAHUAH. Yes, I said my life, my entire will, mind, soul and way of doing things. I have totally yielded myself over to our Heavenly Father YAHUAH's way of doing things. You might ask why. Because I know that He knows best. I have put our Heavenly Father YAHUAH's way to the test, and I come out on top all the time. You know we like success.

Now, we also like power. There is no other power greater than the Word of YAHUAH. Remember, I have tested the Word. This is not hearsay. This is experience. Any failure I have experienced is because I didn't hear clearly, or I didn't wait for clear instructions. It meant something other than what I thought. There is no failure in the Word or in YAHUAH. There is failure only in not hearing completely or in not hearing at all. You have to have patience in what our Heavenly Father YAHUAH is telling you, especially if you are a driven person. It takes time to learn how to follow the direction of The RUACH HA'QODESH, especially when the directions are coming from your wife. Most of the time, my wife has been correct in her understanding. I learned about my wife being a receiver, and that was an enlightening experience for me. When I pray, she gets interpretation and she also gets instruction for me. If your wife is yielded to the will of the Father, she will receive a lot of information for you and your family.

Most of the time when YAHUAH was talking through my wife, I didn't want to hear what she was saying. I wanted YAHUAH to tell me directly, not through her. I thought she was always trying to tell me what to do, and I was not going to let her control me.

The control wasn't coming from her; the control was coming from our Heavenly Father through her. By now I have learned how to listen and listen well when she talks to me, because she just might have the answer I am looking for.

This was YAHUAH's way of helping me listen and be attentive to my wife, and we have developed good communication skills because now I value her.

The Word of YAHUAH has made me feel a tremendous amount of power. This is the true power. The things we should be controlling are our time with our Heavenly Father YAHUAH and our time confessing the Word of YAHUAH. If we do this, our Heavenly Father YAHUAH will control the rest with His direction. We do not have control over our wives. We are to love our wives, value them and respect what they bring into our lives.

We are not to control our money. Our money belongs to our Heavenly Father YAHUAH and again, if we consult Him on what to do, He will give us direction. When I consult our Heavenly Father YAHUAH about how to give, He directs and there is always increase. We are the stewards of YAHUAH's money, and He directs our paths.

I thought I was being a good steward, saving, paying my bills, and taking care of my family, but I didn't even know what a good steward was until our Heavenly Father YAHUAH taught me. Being a good steward means finding out what YAHUAH wants you to do with your money and your time. The only way you can find out is to spend more time with our Heavenly Father YAHUAH. Our Heavenly Father YAHUAH will always have blessing someone in mind. For example, our Heavenly Father YAHUAH had me take someone out to lunch on my birthday.

He had us giving our wedding rings away when we were renewing our marriage vows.

It taught me how to give freely and unconditionally and most of all, I was not tied to material things. It really freed me more and more every time our Heavenly Father YAHUAH had me give something away.

Everything belongs to our Heavenly Father YAHUAH anyway. I have to die to my own desires and my own way of doing things every day and continue to learn how to be a man of YAHUAH.

I had been feeding on the wrong information most of my life. It was not from the mind of YAHUAH, it was from the mind of carnal men. I love learning how our Heavenly Father YAHUAH wants me to respond to things and getting the correct understanding on subjects. It makes me aware of how much more I have to learn. It really is an adventure, and I am loving every minute of it. Our Heavenly Father YAHUAH is so fascinating. There is no end to the wisdom and revelation knowledge He gives me so freely.

Oh, taste and see that YAHUAH is good; Blessed is the man who trusts in Him!
Psalm 34:8 NKJV

"Blessed" means empowered to succeed. "Empowered" suggests that someone else or something empowers you, and that is the power of the Word of YAHUAH manifested in your life.

The reason I feel power inside now is that I am full of the Word of YAHUAH. The Word of YAHUAH brings the power. It is The RUACH YAHUAH that comes upon you in power. Our Heavenly Father YAHUAH is Almighty.

I don't know about you, but I like the real thing. When I speak the Word, I feel the power coming out of me because I abide in the Word of YAHUAH and He abides in me. This causes me to speak with confidence because the authority is in the Word of YAHUAH.

I speak with authority because of the Word of YAHUAH and because The RUACH HA'QODESH leads me in what to say. I do not give people my opinions. I give them only the Word of YAHUAH and what The RUACH HA'QODESH gives revelation to me for them. I have tasted the blessings of YAHUAH, and He has added no sorrow.

I am my wife's covering and she is my glory. That is the mind of YAHUAH, not a carnal mind. Let me give you an example of what I used to think because of what I was told and what I observed. I am sure it will not surprise you.

I used to think a man should work as many hours as it takes to take care of his family. He should get as far and as fast as he can in his career and make as much money as he can. His wife should not complain, because her husband is just doing what a man should do. The wife should cook, clean, and take care of the children. The husband is the boss of his wife and their children. As long as the husband is doing all these things, the wife has nothing to say about it.

For many years, I had been very selfish in my marriage, never giving my wife the opportunity to be heard. I ignored her input. In short, I didn't value her opinion. I would listen but would not take any of her advice.

Our Heavenly Father YAHUAH gave me the revelation on how to treat my wife. He told me to take care of her. He told me the housekeeper was to take care of the house, the nanny should help with the children, and I needed to take care of my wife's needs. Our Heavenly Father YAHUAH let me know she was my responsibility and I needed to make sure she was emotionally taken care of.

The majority of the time, our Heavenly Father YAHUAH would talk to me through my wife. I learned to value her and what she had to say. Our communication developed in such an awesome way. We love to talk with each other now. We both learn from each other and respect each other in a way only our Heavenly Father YAHUAH could have taught us. He taught us to be thankful for each other.

He helped us to complement each other, to respect and love one another. We have such a great relationship now because of our Heavenly Father YAHUAH. I cannot even express in words what our Heavenly Father YAHUAH has done. It is so wonderful. He cares so much for our relationship. our Heavenly Father YAHUAH wants us to cherish and love our relationships with our wives and our children.

I knew it was our Heavenly Father YAHUAH talking through my wife, because I would ask Him a question and He would answer it through my wife even though she didn't know I had even asked our Heavenly Father YAHUAH my question. This happened several times, and I started to pay more and more attention to my wife. We were having three-way conversations.

I would be thinking about something and have a good question for our Heavenly Father YAHUAH. He would answer through my wife and it was startling at first, but I became accustomed to it.

Those experiences let me know, without a shadow of a doubt, that my wife was hearing from Him. I didn't know how I liked the idea of our Heavenly Father YAHUAH sharing my thoughts with her, but I understood why He was doing it this way. I had to know it was our Heavenly Father YAHUAH my wife was hearing from.

This was such an awesome time with our Heavenly Father YAHUAH, and so personal that we could hardly believe YAHUAH would be so personal with us. It is so special. Our Heavenly Father YAHUAH makes us feel so special.

Our Heavenly Father YAHAUH taught me that if I took care of my wife, she would take care of me. That was not the way I had thought before. He taught me that if I wanted to control and dominate something, it should be satan, continuing to reinforce his defeat.

Our Heavenly Father YAHUAH let me know that because of the things we were doing in our lives, my wife needed help with the house and the children. If I wanted my wife there for me, I had to make sure she was rested and able to be there for me.

Our Heavenly Father YAHUAH made sure I knew my wife was not the housekeeper, the babysitter or just there for my needs.

We are a team and we complement each other. We love, cherish, and respect each other's opinion and the call of YAHUAH on our lives. I am not more important than she is. The call on my life is not more important than the call on her life. My wife and I are friends, lovers and partners.

Now that our Heavenly Father YAHUAH has done a mighty work in us, our Heavenly Father YAHUAH said, "You are destined for Greatness."

These are the scriptures He gave us:

Therefore if anyone cleanses himself from the latter, he will be a vessel for honor, sanctified and useful for the Maser, prepared for every good work.
2 Timothy 2:21 NKJV

For we are His workmanship, created in MASHIACH YAHUSHA for good works, which YAHUAH prepared beforehand that we should walk in them.
Ephesians 2:10 NKJV

And He said to them, "Go into all the world and preach the gospel to every creature. He who believes and is baptized will be saved; but he who does not believe will be condemned. And these signs will follow those who believe: In my name they will cast out demons; they will speak with new tongues; They will take up serpents; and if they drink anything deadly, it will by no means hurt them; they will lay hands on the sick, and they will recover."
Mark 16:15-18 NKJV

YAHUSHA said to him, "If you can believe, all things are possible to him who believes."
Mark 9:23 NKJV

Our Heavenly Father YAHUAH is good. He said the hundredfold return for us was to be returned to the position in Genesis 1:27: "So YAHUAH created man in His own image, in the image and likeness of YAHUAH he created him, male and female He created them."

Our Heavenly Father YAHUAH said to Andrea and me, "You have been returned to the Garden of Eden." Glory to YAHUAH! We now walk in the cool of the day with YAHUAH just as Adam and Eve did before they fell and disobeyed YAHUAH and sin separated them from YAHUAH! Thanks to YAHUSHA HA'MASHIACH who died for our sins and restored us back to YAHUAH.

In Him we live and move and have our being, as also some of your own poets have said, "For we are also His offspring."
Acts 17:28 NKJV

If we have not let go of what we thought was a good life, we would have missed all of things we just told you about. Believe me, we didn't have any of these things as our goals. Our Heavenly Father YAHUAH is an awesome ELOHIYM. If you follow Him, His way, you will not be sorry. We certainly are not sorry. We have abundance in a way we could not even have thought of. We have exceedingly, abundantly more than we could have thought or asked. Praise the name of our ADONAI and Savior YAHUSHA HA'MASHIACH.

Chapter Eleven

~ ~ ~ ~ ~ ~ ~ ~ ~

We Are Woke, There Has Been
A Necessary Change

If the son therefore shall make you free ye shall be free
indeed!
John 8:36 KJV

Wow! Return us back to the garden like mentality when we
could talk mouth to mouth with our Heavenly Father
because of YAHUSHA, who became our Savior, our
Master, our Coming King!

Our Heavenly Father YAHUAH started talking to Melvin
and me about why our ministry was called Kingdom
Treasures International and who we really are to Him as
Black people! WE SAID WHAT! BLACK PEOPLE! YOU
ARE ISRAEL, in Hebrew Yisrael, THE PEOPLE OF THE
BIBLE! WHAT! Our Heavenly Father YAHUAH gave us
scripture, after scripture, after scripture and we learned
about the law, statues and commandments.

Here is the patience of the saints; here are those who keep the commandments of YAHUAH and the faith of YAHUSHA.

Revelations 14:12 NKJV

Then here it came, the Truth! We have all been lied to. Questions came, then who are those people in Israel? So, we went to Israel!

"I know your works, tribulation, and poverty (but you are rich); and I know the blasphemy of those who say they are Jews and are not, but are a synagogue of satan.

Revelations 2:9 NKJV

Indeed I will make those of the synagogue of satan, who say they are Jews and are not, but lie—indeed I will make them come and worship before your feet, and to know that I have loved you.

Revelations 3:9 NKJV

Then our Heavenly Father YAHUAH continued showing us and leading us to information, historical documents, and DNA evidence, confirming that the people of the Bible referred to as the children of Israel, were the ancestors of the people that were brought to The United States as slaves, also referred to as negroes! While we were in Israel we went to the desert and talked with the Bedouins People, who were Black Arabs. They told us you are the true Israelites! We are not gentiles! We are our Heavenly Father YAHUAH's chosen people!

Our Heavenly Father YAHUAH spent a lot of time proving to us that we hear from Him accurately and that we love Him unconditionally. We left all to follow Him! We were not with Him for material possession. We passed the rich young ruler in the Bible test.

Now behold, one came and said to Him, "Good Teacher, what good thing shall I do that I may have eternal life?"

So He said to him, "Why do you call Me good? No one is good but One, that is, YAHUAH. But if you want to enter into life, keep the commandments."

He said to Him, "Which ones?"

YAHUSHA said, "'You shall not murder,' 'You shall not commit adultery,' 'You shall not steal,' 'You shall not bear false witness,' 'Honor your father and your mother,' and, 'You shall love your neighbor as yourself.'"

The young man said to Him, "All these things I have kept from my youth. What do I still lack?"

YAHUSHA said to him, "If you want to be perfect, go, sell what you have and give to the poor, and you will have treasure in heaven; and come, follow Me."

But when the young man heard that saying, he went away sorrowful, for he had great possessions.
Matthew 19:16-22 NKJV

What we wanted and desired was a relationship with Him, and we had one with Him. Our Heavenly Father YAHUAH is now giving us the fullness of the love relationship He has with Israel and this group called Judah! Yehuda in Hebrew! YAHUAH led us to scriptures and information that proved He was not a blue eye, blond hair Caucasian! Oh my goodness! He proved it to us through scriptures that this was all true! Our Savior and Master and Our Coming King's Name is YAHUSHA, My Redeemer, and He is Black!

saying, "I am the Alpha and the Omega, the First and the Last," and, "What you see, write in a book and send it to the seven churches which are in Asia: to Ephesus, to Smyrna, to Pergamos, to Thyatira, to Sardis, to Philadelphia, and to Laodicea."

Then I turned to see the voice that spoke with me. And having turned I saw seven golden lampstands, and in the midst of the seven lampstands One like the Son of Man, clothed with a garment down to the feet and girded about the chest with a golden band. His head and hair were white like wool, as white as snow, and His eyes like a flame of fire; His feet were like fine brass, as if refined in a furnace, and His voice as the sound of many waters; He had in His right hand seven stars, out of His mouth went a sharp two-edged sword, and His countenance was like the sun shining in its strength. And when I saw Him, I fell at His feet as dead. But He laid His right hand on me, saying to me, "Do not be afraid; I am the First and the Last. I am He who lives, and was dead, and behold, I am alive forevermore. Amen. And I have the keys of Hades and of Death.
Revelations 1:11-18 NKJV

The climate was changing on the earth and Nikole Hannah-Jones a staff writer for the New York Times Magazine talked about the 1619 Project! Then the violent murder of George Floyd by a white police officer happened! NOW MELVIN WILL TALK TO YOU ABOUT WHY BLACK LIVES MATTER!

For nothing is secret that will not be revealed,

nor anything hidden that will not be known and come to

light.

Luke 8:17 NKJV

WE HAVE ALL BEEN LIED TO!

When our Heavenly Father YAHUAH awakened me and

my family to the truth of who we are, the chosen people of

our Heavenly Father YAHUAH, Israel, His holy people, a

special treasure above all the peoples of the face of the

earth as is written in Deuteronomy 7:6, I knew right away

as He spoke, that it was the undeniable truth. It hit my

ruach, with force. As a Black man growing up in the

United States, it answered every question that I ever had

about our people being brought here as slaves and stolen

from our homeland. Questions like, why were we given a

lifestyle of savagery, brutal existence, and inhumane

conditions for over two hundred forty years? And why,

even to this date has inequality, injustices across the board

and yes systemic racism, plagued our people?

Now when I look at the Bible, I'm looking at it as our

history book, and most of the characters are black. I'm

excited about the Bible like never before. It is a book that really gives me more than just hope, it gives me the reality of who I am. Reading it excites my ruach.

When I read all of Deuteronomy chapter 28, automatically the Word jumps out at me while reading the blessings and curses. I can see that it's so plain that we fit the narrative of the scripture. No other people completely fit the book like Black people in America and besides that our Heavenly Father YAHUAH said so! We are His people!

As we came into the year 2019, the 1619 project was released. The 1619 Project is an ongoing initiative from The New York Times Magazine that began in August 2019, the 400th anniversary of the beginning of American slavery. It aims to reframe the country's history by placing the consequences of slavery and the contributions of black Americans at the very center of our national narrative. I find it also interesting that our Heavenly Father YAHUAH decided that 2019 would be the year He would completely lift the curse off His people. He spoke that to us. We as a people must repent and return to Him.

In February 2020, our Heavenly Father YAHUAH led us to go to the celebration of Africatown, a suburb in Mobile, Alabama. We went to Africatown to see and hear the descendants from the last slaves that were brought to America illegally, in 1860, on a ship called the Clotilda. National Geographic was also in Africatown at this time documenting the story. As part of Nat Geo's involvement, their team of underwater archeologists found the remains of the Clotilda along the shore of Alabama's Mobile River. Nat Geo also did an article in their magazine in February 2020 to honor the lives of the Black slaves that were illegally taken. In 1808, importing slaves to The United States was outlawed, but during a heated argument, a slave owner, made a wager that he could bring slaves to The United States without being noticed. Once the slaves reached Alabama, and the cargo was taken off the ship, they burned the ship in order to hide the evidence. It was a very humbling experience to listen to brothers and sisters who can actually trace the place and time when their ancestors were brought to this country.

As I continued to read and research things about my people, I came across another one of America's original sins that had long been forgotten. It is called the Devil's Punch Bowl, and it occurred in Natchez, Mississippi after the civil war. Black people in that area that were recently freed from slavery, with no place to go, found their way to the city of Natchez. The population grew from 10,000 people to 120,000 people almost overnight. In order to deal with the population influx of recently freed slaves, a concentration camp was established to essentially eradicate the freed slaves. The men were recaptured by the Union Troops and forced back into hard labor. The women and children were locked behind the concrete walls of the camp and left to die from starvation. Many also died from the smallpox disease. In total over 20,000 freed slaves were killed in one year. When I heard about this my heart sunk. I knew at that moment by my ruach, some of my ancestors died in that hell hole, because Natchez, Mississippi is the place of my birth. They didn't receive any direction or help from The United States government. It's really amazing that our people survived such cruelty by White America.

I found myself on a journey with my wife also. Our Heavenly Father YAHUAH would take us around the city to different restaurants and stores blessing White gentiles. As He was leading us to bless people who had need of money, we would leave large tips at restaurants or give in other ways while we were out.

We asked our Heavenly Father YAHUAH why did He have us do all those things for White gentiles. He said that was His way of preventing bitterness and hatred from entering into our hearts. Praise our Heavenly Father YAHUAH! One thing when being led of The RUACH is always remember, our Heavenly Father YAHUAH's ways are higher than our ways.

"For My thoughts are not your thoughts,
Nor are your ways My ways," says YAHUAH.
"For as the heavens are higher than the earth,
So are My ways higher than your ways,
And My thoughts than your thoughts
Isaiah 55:8-9 NKJV

Our Heavenly Father continued to give us much revelation all the time, face to face. Along with revealing our identity our Heavenly Father YAHUAH also revealed His name that we were praying and asking for. YAHUAH is the Father's name and YAHUSHA HA'MASHIACH is the Son's name!

It had been years of praying and seeking our Heavenly Father YAHUAH for His timing for our mission trip to India. Finally, the time came in 2020. My wife and I went there with the gospel which had not been preached with their true names. I could feel the difference when we preached. The power was greater, and felt more comfortable in the Anointing. People were repenting and asking for forgiveness. We preached The Kingdom of YAHUAH to Hindus and Muslims, which compelled people to go home after service and throw away their idols of other gods.

As Israelites, it's time for us to repent to our Heavenly Father (YAHUAH), take our place, start listening and being led of The RUACH, yield ourselves to Him, submit to His will and Obey His Word. We are the people that must be in place to usher in the Messiah, The King of Kings, YAHUSHA HA'MASHIACH.

THIS IS WHY BLACK LIVES MATTER!

WE ARE THE PEOPLE OF THE HOLY BIBLE!

So Samuel said:

"Has YAHUAH as great delight in burnt offerings and sacrifices,
As in obeying the voice of YAHUAH?
Behold, to obey is better than sacrifice,
And to heed than the fat of rams.
1 Samuel 15:22 NKJV

But this is what I commanded them, saying, 'Obey My voice, and I will be your ELOHIYM, and you shall be My people. And walk in all the ways that I have commanded you, that it may be well with you.'
Jeremiah 7:23 NKJV

Put On The New Man

that, regarding your previous way of life, you put off your old self [completely discard your former nature], which is being corrupted through deceitful desires, and
be continually renewed in the ruach of your mind [having a fresh, untarnished mental and spiritual attitude], and put on the new self [the regenerated and renewed nature], created in YAHUAH's image, in the righteousness and holiness of the truth [living in a way that expresses to YAHUAH your gratitude for your salvation].
Ephesians 4:22-24 AMP

Be Strong In YAHUAH

In conclusion, be strong in YAHUAH [draw your strength from Him and be empowered through your union with Him] and in the power of His [boundless] might. Ephesians 6:10 AMP

SAY THEIR NAMES

Call on the name of our Father YAHUAH and our Savior YAHUSHA and the Power of The RUACH HA'QODESH.

SINNER'S PRAYER

Oh YAH in Heaven, I come to you. I confess I have not lived my life for you. I am a sinner; I need remission of my sins and I have need of a savior. Right now I repent of my sins, and renounce satan and all other gods as my ELOHIYM. I believe you sent YAHUSHA to die for me and on the third day you raised Him from the dead and He now sits at the right hand of YAHUAH. YAHUSHA, you are the son of YAH. Come into my life and be my ADONAI and Savior. And by the power of the RUACH HA'QODESH, I will live my life for you. Amen.

Congratulations!!! If you just said the prayer above for the first time, we believe you are born again from above, a new creation. Welcome to the family of YAHUAH!!!

But there's far more to life for us. We're citizens of high heaven! We're waiting the arrival of the Savior, the Master, YAHUSHA HA'MASHIACH, who will transform our earthy bodies into glorious bodies like his own. He'll make us beautiful and whole with the same powerful skill by which he is putting everything as it should be, under and around him.
Philippians 3:20-21 MSG

SHALOM!

About The Authors

Dr. Melvin C. Rhines, Sr. and Dr. Andrea P. Rhines are pastors and founders of the Assembly of Kingdom Treasures International, a place where groups of people from all ethnicities gather to learn the truth. They have been in ministry since 1998 and answered the call of YAHUAH on their lives to pastor in 2001. It was not until 1998, when Dr. Melvin C. Rhines, Sr. received the baptism of The RUACH HA'QAODESH with the evidence of speaking in tongues (Heavenly Language), that revelation knowledge of YAHUAH's Word changed his life, and has continued to increase the lives of the people that they minister to. Dr. Melvin C. Rhines, Sr. attributes the success of their lives and ministry to having an intimate relationship with YAHUAH and YAHUSHA HA'MASHIACH, dedication, obedience, discipline to the voice of YAHUAH, and being led by The RUACH HA'QODESH.

But you, beloved, build yourselves up on [the foundation of] your most holy faith [continually progress, rise like an edifice higher and higher], pray in The RUACH HA'QODESH, and keep yourselves in the love of

YAHUAH, waiting anxiously and looking forward to the mercy of our ADONAI YAHUSHA HA'MASHIACH [which will bring you] to eternal life.

Jude 1:20-21 AMP

As a pilot, Dr. Melvin C. Rhines Sr. loves to fly both airplanes and helicopters. He also enjoys scuba diving, riding motorcycles, golf, deep-sea fishing and ice fishing. Dr. Andrea Rhines also enjoys flying with Dr. Melvin C. Rhines Sr. and going on motorcycle rides with him. She enjoys snorkeling and singing songs from Heaven to her Heavenly Father. Most of all they love to read the Bible and pray with their children and grandchildren.

To contact Dr. Melvin C. Rhines Sr.
and Dr. Andrea P. Rhines:

Assembly of Kingdom Treasures International

PO Box 44263

Eden Prairie, MN 55344

(952) 239-1342

You can also visit their ministry's website at:

www.kingdomtreasuresintl.com

www.ingramcontent.com/pod-product-compliance
Lightning Source LLC
LaVergne TN
LVHW011329080426
835513LV00006B/253